THE ST. LOUIS JESUITS

Thirty Years

To Barb,

May God be our hope.

Dan Schutte

Barb – God bless you!

Yours Truly,

Roc O'Connor

Bob Dufford SJ

Tim Manion

THE ST. LOUIS JESUITS

Thirty Years

CELEBRATING THE WORK OF FIVE GIFTED

COMPOSERS AND THE CONTRIBUTION

THEY'VE MADE TO THE PRAYER AND

WORSHIP OF CHRISTIANS

Edited by Mike Gale

Edition 6144
ISBN 1-56929-074-1

© 2006, Mike Gale
Published by Oregon Catholic Press
5536 NE Hassalo Street
Portland, OR 97213
Phone: 800-LITURGY (548-8749)
Fax: (503) 282-3486
E-mail: liturgy@ocp.org
Web site: ocp.org
All rights reserved.
Printed in Mexico.

Editor: Mike Gale
Publisher: John J. Limb
Director of Editorial Processes Division: Victor Cozzoli
Managing Editor: Eric Schumock
Project Editor: Bari Colombari
Editing Assistance: Mónica Rodríguez
Project Consultant: Jean Germano
Graphic Layout: Dan Schutte
Layout Consultant: Susan Irish
Cover Design: Susan Irish
Cover Photo: Le Vu

Cover: Upper image (l. to r.) — Dan Schutte, Bob Dufford, S.J., John Foley, S.J., Tim Manion, Roc O'Connor, S.J.
Lower image (back) Roc O'Connor, S.J., Tim Manion, (front) Bob Dufford, S.J., Dan Schutte, John Foley S.J.

Acknowledgements:

With special thanks to Bob Dufford S.J., John Foley S.J., Tim Manion, Roc O'Connor S.J. and Dan Schutte for contributing their treasure of photographs and their reflections on their thirty years of service to the prayer of Christian people. Also with great appreciation to Jim McDermott, S.J., writer for *America* magazine, for allowing us to use the material he collected and wrote during his interviews with the St. Louis Jesuits. Thanks to Debbie McAuliffe for her hours of research and compilation assistance. And finally, with much appreciation to the bishops, publishers, colleagues and friends who shared their personal stories and offered their expressions of gratitude for the music of these men.

(RRDSC0106)

Introduction

Musical liturgy is normative, formative and transformative. From my perspective as president of the National Association of Pastoral Musicians, the St. Louis Jesuits played a decisive role in the development of liturgical music and liturgical theology in the United States and in implementing the renewal of the Second Vatican Council (1962–1965). The Saint Louis Jesuits: Thirty Years helps to identify their contribution.

We've all prayed with their music, and so we know the gift it offers. With this book, we catch a glimpse of the composers and their texts, both then and now. Unless you were a part of the scene, it is hard to imagine those early years.

Thirty years ago, the music of the 60s was everywhere and seeping from radios and into parish repertoires. The music of College Chapel at St. Louis University in the early 70s was different and it reached people by word of mouth, memory and mimeograph machines. This music spread because it was better than what was being sung: it was more scriptural, filled with more powerful biblical images and deeper theological insights and, above all, was well-crafted music immanently able to be sung by a congregation. By singing psalms, we learned that musical liturgy is normative, and it became obvious to everyone that the Christian church wanted to sing psalms.

Not only did parish musicians instantly recognize the uniqueness of this music, so did parishioners. They sang it, and they wanted to sing it again and again. By singing it, the entire American church changed, and not only musically; the faithful's understanding of God, the church, and the call of God was transformed. Musical liturgy is formative.

The deep religious convictions that brought these gifted men together are still apparent in their lives. I am proud to call them my friends. The group they formed was named by their first publisher, Ray Bruno.

In "Berkeley and Beyond," you will be surprised at how reluctant they were to become a group. While reticent to become a performing group, they did discover the importance of group composition. By critiquing one another's work, sometimes with painful honesty, they learned from one another, uncovering some principles of congregational singing: clear entrances, correct range and anticipated melodies.

As you read "Then and Now" and "Music of the Soul," you'll experience their own reflections on their favorite texts. Take some time to pray again with these texts. They capture the spirit of the Second Vatican Council: the ecstatic jubilation of liberation ("Sing a New Song"), the hope for unity of all ("One Bread, One Body") and the call for justice (in the text "Gentile or Jew, …woman or man, no more").

There is a gift in these texts; each one of us has experienced it. The truths of our believing, trusting and questioning our religious inheritance are in all our hearts, and with these songs they can be sung out loud in our worship. We find a way to join our voices together in recognition of the God present with us ("Yahweh, I know you are near") and the call to serve others ("Here I am, Lord" and "… I will hold your people in my heart"). As you read the composers' own reflections and insights into the texts, take time to be touched by them again. *The St. Louis Jesuits: Thirty Years* can make these texts live again in your heart. Musical liturgy is transformative.

The St. Louis Jesuits were present at the first convention of the National Association of Pastoral Musicians in 1978 in Scranton, and they gathered again at the twenty-fifth anniversary in Washington, DC, in 2001. Both experiences were memorable. In "Time for Reunion," you will see the fruit of their labor: a new recording.

The St. Louis Jesuits were important contributors to the development of liturgical renewal in the Catholic Church in the United States. Not only did they provide music to sing at worship but, even more importantly, they provided a way for the best truths of the Catholic Church to be internalized by everyone who sang them. Thirty years ago, the St. Louis Jesuits, filled with the hopes of the Second Vatican Council, began to create a means for the entire American church to pray this vision. Today, people still want to sing these truths. The St. Louis Jesuits bring you a "Vision of Hope."

Rev. Virgil C. Funk
President Emeritus,
National Association of Pastoral Musicians

In the Light of Vatican II

"Illuminated by the light of this Council, the Church — we confidently trust — will become greater in spiritual riches and, gaining the strength of new energies therefore, she will look upon the future without fear. In fact, by bringing herself up-to-date where required, and by the wise organization of mutual cooperation, the Church will make men, families and peoples really turn their minds to heavenly things.

The Council now beginning rises in the Church like daybreak, a forerunner of the most splendid light. It is now only dawn and already, at this first announcement of the rising day, how much sweetness fills our heart. Everything here breathes sanctity and arouses great joy. Let us contemplate the stars, which with their brightness augment the majesty of this temple. These stars, according to the testimony of the Apostle John (Revelation 1:20), are you, and with you we see shining around the tomb of the Prince of the Apostles, the golden candelabra, that is, the church is confided to you (Revelation).

We might say that heaven and earth are united in the holding of the Council — the saints of heaven to protect our work, the faithful of the earth continuing in prayer to the Lord, and you, seconding the inspiration of the Holy Spirit in order that the work of all may correspond to the modern expectations and needs of the various peoples of the world.

God grant that your labors and your work, toward which the eyes of all peoples and hopes of the entire world are turned, may abundantly fulfill the aspirations of all."

Pope John XXIII, Opening Address of Second Vatican Council on October 11, 1962

September 10, 2005

Dan Schutte
Composer in Residence
University of San Francisco
2130 Fulton Street
San Francisco, CA 94117

Dear Mr. Schutte,

It has been brought to my attention that you, Father Robert Dufford, S.J.,
Father Robert O'Connor, S.J., and Father John Foley, S.J., are celebrating
the anniversary of your collaborative ministry in music as the "St. Louis
Jesuits." For over thirty years you have blessed the worship of people
all over the world with your beautiful hymns. Through my connection
with Oregon Catholic Press, I am well aware of how many worshipping
communities continue to use your songs in various liturgical settings.

You have made a great and lasting contribution to the liturgical life of the
Church. Many have noted favorably the way in which you have drawn
from and developed Scriptural themes in your music. We are grateful
to you and ask that God will bless you all with health and continued
inspiration. Congratulations as you celebrate this thirtieth anniversary!

Sincerely yours in Christ,

The Most Reverend William J. Levada
Archbishop Emeritus of San Francisco
Prefect, Congregation for the Doctrine of the Faith

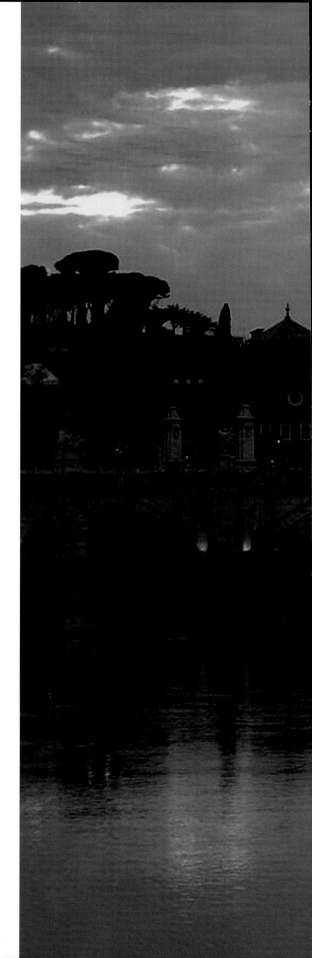

St. Peter's Basilica in Rome

Curia Generalizia della Compagnia di Gesù
Borgo S. Spirito, 4
C.P. 6139 / 00195 ROMA-PRATI (Italia)
Tel . 06/689.771 _ Fax 06/686.8214

August 5, 2005

Rev. Robert Dufford, S.J.
Rev. John Foley, S.J.
Rev. Robert O'Connor, S.J.
Mr. Daniel Schutte

Dear Brothers in the Lord,

With great pleasure and pride I write to honor you, the Saint Louis Jesuits, on the occasion of the thirty-year celebration of your accomplishments and contributions to the liturgical life of the Church throughout the world. Your creativity and dedication have helped to bring church music to the people and the people to church music. I am sure that I join many others in recognizing this wonderful gift of the Spirit through your special talents and prayerful devotion.

In my travels around the world I have seen how your songs have reached the far corners of the earth and are sung all over the globe, even by many for whom English is not a spoken language. You have been a source of grace for many believers in fostering the liturgical renewal to which the Second Vatican Council called us. Faithful to the spirit of Saint Ignatius, your gifts have inspired many to live and labor for the greater glory of God.

May God's Spirit continue to bless you and your work.

Sincerely in Christ

Peter-Hans Kolvenbach, S.J.
Superior General

Peter-Hans Kolvenbach, S.J., Superior General of the Society of Jesus, 1983 to present

Bishops gathered in St. Peter's Basilica in Rome during Second Vatican Council

"The vision of Vatican II focussed on liturgical worship as the principal expression of our faith. As we pray, so we believe. The St Louis Jesuits through their music and song enliven our journey as People of God. I am grateful for their ministry, which enriches our heritage. By helping us to share more fruitfully in the divine liturgy, they broaden and deepen our relationship with God. They enable us to claim and celebrate more fully the joy and justice of the divine Reign."

Bishop Remi J. De Roo
Retired Bishop of Victoria, Canada
Council Father at Vatican II

"Among the many signs and symbols used by the Church to celebrate its faith, music is of preeminent importance," says *Music in Catholic Worship* published by the Bishops of the United States in 1983. Since the renewal of the Order of Mass following Vatican II, the ministry of the composer has been critical in creating a vernacular style of liturgical music that both engages the assembly and supports the Eucharistic ritual in keeping with the directives of the Constitution on the Sacred Liturgy. The St. Louis Jesuits have ably and superbly helped us along this path. Congratulations on 30 years of ministry! You are a great blessing to the Church.

Most Reverend Donald W. Trautman, STD, SSL
Bishop of Erie, Pennsylvania
Chairman of US Bishops' Committee on the Liturgy

In the Spirit of Ignatius

Ignatius of Loyola (1491–1556), a young Basque soldier wounded in battle and moved by God to transform his life into one of service and love, became the inspiration for these five composers. God took Inigo, as he was called, and taught him like a schoolmaster lovingly teaches his student. It was a  long pilgrimage that would lead Ignatius from his family estate to a cave outside the city of Manresa, from days of study in Paris to the small chapel of La Storta outside Rome. The Society of Jesus was born when Ignatius and nine companions vowed to spend their lives seeking the greater glory of God.

"The Spiritual Journey of St. Ignatius Loyola,"
Panel #5, acrylic on wood panel with gold leaf

We should recall that mediocrity has no place in Ignatius' world view. …He urges us to work for the greater glory of God because the world desperately needs men and women of competence and conscience who generously give of themselves for others.

Peter-Hans Kolvenbach, S.J., Superior General of the Society of Jesus

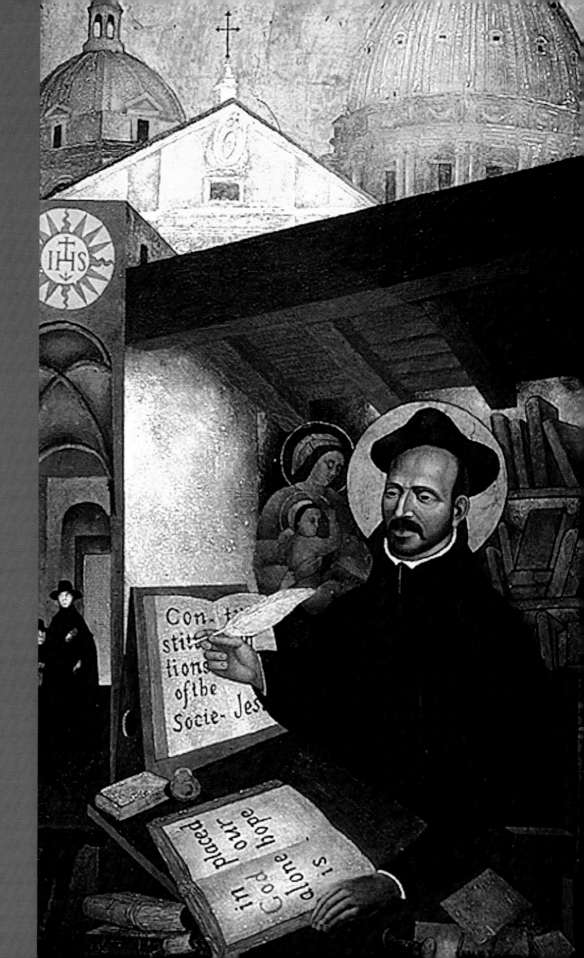

In the things of God, those who are over prudent will hardly ever achieve anything really great. Those who are constantly brooding and vacillating, because they fear the possible outcomes which they foresee, will never turn their hearts towards things of real beauty.

Ignatius of Loyola

Thirty Years Ago

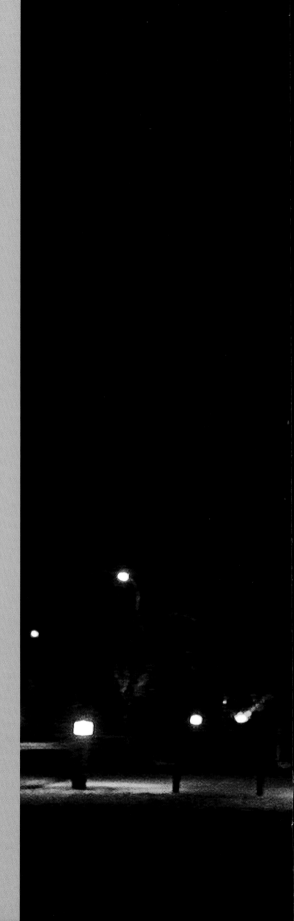

Berkeley, California 1974

Toronto, Ontario 1978

*O*ver thirty years ago, five young men responded with passion and generosity to the challenge set forth by the Second Vatican Council: renewing and adapting the liturgy of the church to modern times. These men — Bob Dufford, John Foley, Tim Manion, Roc O'Connor and Dan Schutte — were attending the University of St. Louis as part of their Jesuit training. Bob Dufford and John Foley were in their theology studies, part of their immediate preparation for ordination; Tim Manion, Roc O'Connor and Dan Schutte were studying philosophy, a series of courses required of all Jesuits.

They didn't have any grand plan in mind but simply tried, each in his own way and in his own time, to respond to the urgings of the Spirit. The beginnings were very simple. Along with other Jesuits, they played and sang for campus liturgies at

St. Louis, Missouri 1993

Meeting with OCP Publisher, John Limb, Portland, Oregon 2004

College Church and Fusz Memorial, the Jesuit House of Studies. As they listened to their hearts, they were inspired to write music in a more popular, contemporary style, and hoped that these pieces would become a way for people to pray.

These inspired liturgies grew to be widely known throughout the St. Louis area, and people came from all over the city to worship on the campus. Many found that the music of these men helped them pray in a way they had not experienced before. The beautiful and singable melodies helped people feel that this music belonged to them. The pieces were easy to learn, but one didn't tire of singing them. The lyrics, drawn from Scripture, allowed people to sing wholeheartedly because the words expressed the prayer of every human heart.

St. Francis Xavier College Church in
St. Louis, Missouri

Fusz Memorial Chapel,
St. Louis, Missouri c. 1960,
presently the Museum
of Christian Art at
St. Louis University

Fusz Memorial Chapel
c. 1960, St. Louis, Missouri

*B*efore the days of photocopy machines, computers, and digital scanners, one used what now seem to be rather primitive ways of making multiple copies of anything. One of those methods involved making a stencil that was then attached to the drum of a ditto machine. The drum was filled with a very flammable, intoxicating fluid that reacted with the resin on the stencil and produced copies of a purple (thus the nickname "purple poop") hue. While quite economical among the available copy methods, the great disadvantage of this system was that a stencil only lasted for about 40 copies before fading in intensity. If a person required 100 copies of something, they would have to make three such stencils in order to accommodate that number.

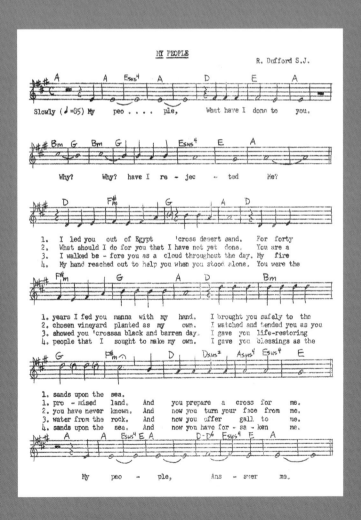

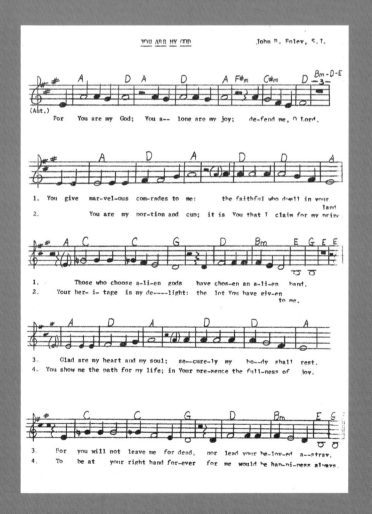

This was the method employed by the St. Louis Jesuits when they first began composing for liturgy. During those years, hundred of such stencils were engraved — each staff line drawn, each note hand drawn, each word carefully typed — to provide copies for the hundreds of people who came to worship at Fusz Memorial and St. Francis Xavier College Church.

Pictured below are some copies of music printed with this method. These are some of the Jesuits' earliest songs. "My People" and "For You Are My God" both were later published in *Neither Silver Nor Gold.* The setting of the "Hail Mary" has never been published.

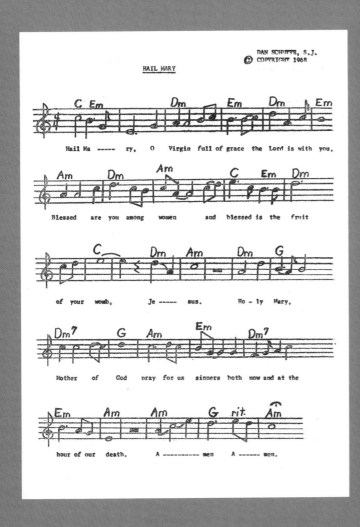

*B*efore coming to St. Louis, Bob Dufford, John Foley and Dan Schutte had been writing liturgical pieces on their own. Although they had never met, John Foley's early works, such as "For You Are My God" and "Rise Up, Jerusalem," had inspired Bob and Dan to write music in a similar style. They brought these with them to St. Louis when they arrived for study.

During the St. Louis years, Bob and Dan convened regularly to offer each other encouragement and critiques of the music they were writing. In early 1972, they discussed the possibility of offering people a bound copy of the music they had written; it would be much more convenient than handing people separate pieces. They discussed the idea with John Foley, John Kavanaugh and Tim Manion, who agreed it would be a wonderful resource to make the music available.

When they pooled their music, they discovered they had fifty-seven pieces. They then set off to create a songbook and record the pieces to demonstrate the feel of the music for other musicians.

Chicago, Illinois 1979

Sing a New Song

♩ = 132   Based on Psalm 98
joyfully, with spirit

Dan Schutte, S.J.

Ant: Sing a new song un-to the Lord; let your song be sung from moun-tains high.

Sing a new song un-to the Lord, sing-ing al-le-lu - ia. _____

1. Yah - weh's peo - ple dance for joy. O come be - fore the
2. Rise, O child - ren, from your sleep; your Sa - vior now has
3. Glad my soul for I have seen the glo - ry of the

1. Lord.__ And play for Him on glad tam - bou - rines, and
2. come.__ He has turned your sor - row to joy, and
3. Lord.__ The trum - pet sounds; the dead shall be raised. I

1. let your trum - pet sound.____ (Antiphon)
2. filled your soul with song.____ (Antiphon)
3. know my Sa - vior lives.____ (Antiphon)

*D*uring his free time, Dan Schutte collected the scores from each composer and began hand-scripting the pieces for a songbook. These were the days before computer notation programs and there weren't funds available to have the scores professionally engraved. In the end, there were 107 pages of music and chord charts. This same year, the others began the process of recording the songs.

They decided they wanted other musicians and singers to hear from the composer the original intent for how a piece should sound. So they set about the task of making a simple recording of their works. Some of these recordings were done in the basement studio at Fusz Memorial, some in the living room of the family of fellow Jesuit and pianist Ralph Caccioppo. Others were recorded live during Fusz chapel liturgies. In the end, the final thirty pieces were recorded in four days in a small, commercial basement studio out in the suburbs. When the recordings were complete, Bob Dufford and John Foley spent two weeks at the studio editing and sequencing the songs for the album.

The singers and musicians for this first collection of songs were fellow Jesuits and university friends, all of whom gave many hours of their time so that this music might become available to people. There were no fees paid for their services. All these people had experienced the power of this music to bring people closer to God and wanted this power to reach even greater numbers. Their playing and singing were labors of loving service to the people of God.

Chicago, Illinois 1979

My relationship with the St. Louis Jesuits began in 1972, I think. My husband, Joe, was stationed at Scott Air Force Base, across the river from St. Louis in Illinois. When we got to Scott in 1969, the charismatic movement was beginning in the area. We had Catholic and Protestant chaplains involved, and the music was a blend of standard hymns with an occasional contemporary piece (e.g., "God is Love").

One Sunday, we decided to attend the basement Mass at St. Louis University. I can't remember how we heard about it, but it had something to do with the music. At that liturgy, the St. Louis Jesuits came into our lives. I didn't realize it at the time, but that first liturgy awakened in us something that had been there all along. The music helped it emerge and grow. It was a real understanding and involvement in the eucharistic celebration as an adult. There must be thousands of others who have experienced similar enlightenment thanks to the way the St. Louis Jesuits shared their gifts over the years.

— **Excerpt from a letter to the St. Louis Jesuits, May 2005**

Chicago, Illinois 1979

I first encountered the music of some young seminarians — sheets of music, ditto-machined and dog-eared copies with penciled-in revisions — when I was assigned to our Jesuit novitiate in Minnesota in 1968. Their music gave life to Scripture and liturgical texts. A few short years later, the corpus of the music, now joined with that of others in St. Louis, enlivened the prayer and worship of many. I easily recommended the Wisconsin Province Jesuits to financially support the first recordings. Why was it an easy recommendation? The music was a great gift to me and, now, to so many others as well.

Fr. Jack Zuercher, S.J.
Regional Assistant, Christian Life Community
Former Assistant Provincial of the Wisconsin Province of the Society of Jesus

31

They wondered how, after they all left St. Louis for other works, their book of songs and recording would be distributed. Unbeknownst by the other, both John Foley and Dan Schutte had submitted their music to several publishers. The response they received was similar: "The music is good but we're not in a position to publish it at this time."

During this same period, the head of a new publishing company, North American Liturgy Resources (NALR), heard about the Jesuit music coming from St. Louis and contacted John Foley. When John told Ray Bruno, the president of NALR, about the Jesuit project, Ray immediately offered to help print, manufacture and distribute the book and recording. Rather than typeset the music for such a large number of pieces, NALR decided to simply photograph the handwritten scores that Dan had inscribed. This compilation of fifty-seven liturgical songs by the Jesuits in St. Louis became their first recorded collection, *Neither Silver Nor Gold*.

The Jesuit composers never gave much thought to what would happen next. There were no plans for more music or other recordings. Dan and Roc left to teach on the Lakota Sioux reservation in South Dakota, while Bob Dufford went to teach at Creighton Preparatory School in Omaha. John Foley stayed in St. Louis as a member of the Jesuit formation team at Fusz Memorial. Tim had already left the Jesuit order by then and was living and going to school in St. Louis.

Berkeley,
California 1974

"I have neither silver nor gold, but what I have I will give you."
Acts of the Apostles 3:5

American churches have relied much on the translated talents of European composers for solidly biblical hymns which invite congregational participation. Such music has served as a bridge over the artifical gaps felt between traditional hymns and various "contemporary" styles of song for worship.

With the publication of NEITHER SILVER NOR GOLD, seeds planted in the American heartland over a decade ago have yielded a rich and mature harvest. Widespread acclaim for the liturgical music of "the St. Louis Jesuits" was heard long before North American Liturgy Resources itself was established. During that era in which many popularized liturgical songs were tried, liked or vehemently disliked, worn out or abused, frozen or discarded, men of the Jesuit community in Saint Louis were steadily and surely developing a fresh tradition of liturgical song which was faithful to the riches of Scripture and the liturgical seasons, but which also responded to the need for vitality in musical style and more varied and authentic instrumental accompaniment in public worship.

Antagonisms rooted in musical taste or prejudice are melted away by the integrity of these compositions, thoroughly tried by time and use. This well-developed library of music for all the seasons of worship offers sung prayers which are as appropriate for cathedral celebrations as they are meaningful for upper room gatherings. Throughout this 55-title repertoire, the guitar has frequent opportunity for moments of majesty . . . the full potential of the great organ is made welcome . . . ordinary people discover they can sing beautiful harmony . . . the words of Scripture are indeed for today . . . the oft-discouraged SATB choir becomes integral to the most contemporary of celebrations.

All music has power. Bad music is incredibly destructive. Mediocre music dulls the spirit. We are convinced that the varied repertoire provided by this monumental publishing-recording project contains a Power of healing, of encouragement, of re-kindling.

No amount of silver, nor any treasury of gold, can give to the Church the kind of Richness offered by these new hymns and psalms.

JOHN FOLEY, S.J.

St. Louis Jesuits

BOB DUFFORD, S.J.

DAN SCHUTTE, S.J.

JOHN KAVANAUGH, S.J.

TIM MANION, S.J.

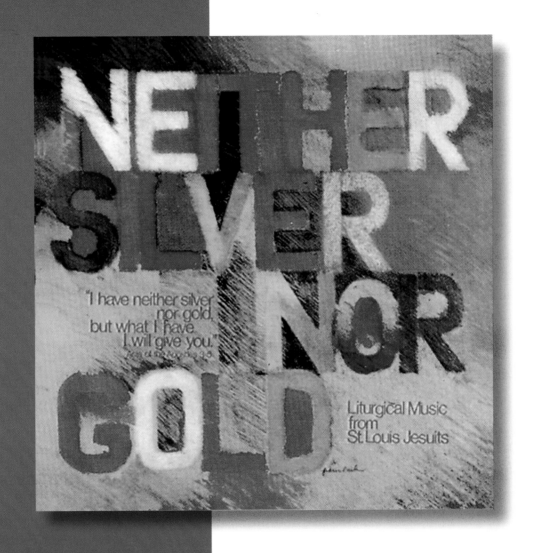

CURIA PRÆPOSITI GENERALIS

SOCIETATIS IESU

ROMA - Borgo S. Spirito, 5

Rome, october 11, 1974

The Rev. John B. Foley
St. Louis - U.S.A.

Dear Father Foley,   Pax Christi.

I cannot very well write to "the St. Louis Jesuits", and so
I am writing them through you, to thank all of you for sending me
neither gold nor silver, but what you have, your fine collection
of liturgical music, and also for your earlier album with "Ways
to get through".

What you have, and what you sent me is indeed of very great
value, especially as a testimony of Christian faith, presented in
beautiful lyrical compositions, and it is no wonder that earlier
antagonisms and prejudice have melted away.

I would hope that through your music and song, which are
such powerful means of communication, many will walk more steadily.
Not through gifts of gold and silver, but through what you have to
give.

With repeated thanks, and with a promise of prayers for you
and your work, I am

Devotedly yours in Christ,

Pedro Arrupe, S.J.

Pedro Arrupe, S.J. was the Superior General of the Society of Jesus from 1965-1981

The last area of liturgical reform to achieve anything approaching lasting quality is that of liturgical music. ...For the adult liturgical assembly, it is difficult to imagine anything that presently surpasses the liturgical music of the St. Louis Jesuits.

Their song book and record album, *Neither Silver Nor Gold*, is, in my opinion, the most consistently high-level collection of liturgical songs now in use. The lyrics tend to be either directly scriptural or very closely tied to Scripture, and are almost without exception, not only poetic but intelligible. It is a pleasure to have at our disposal a collection of hymns which are theologically unobjectionable. The music has that possibility of permanence that only comes about through the right mixture of sophistication and immediate attractiveness.

— **Review by James L. Empereur, S.J.**
   for *Celebration* magazine, 1974

*T*he Jesuits faced the challenge of finding a piece of art for the cover of their first book and record. They didn't have to look far for an artist who knew their music and understood their purpose. When they approached Donald-David Fehrenbach, a fellow Jesuit and artist who lived with Dan and Roc at Fusz Memorial, he could not have been more gracious in accepting the task of creating a piece of art for the cover of *Neither Silver Nor Gold.*

Over the years, Donald-David painted the cover art for all but the last of St. Louis Jesuit recording, *The Steadfast Love*, recorded in 1985. The most extraordinary and amazingly generous element of Donald-David's process was that each time he created several pieces so the Jesuits would be able to choose from among them the one they liked best. They wanted the cover art to express the character of the music. The cover for them was really an extension of the music in visual form. When people saw the cover of the album, they wanted the artwork to draw people in to the music.

Donald-David was called home to God on April 10, 1998, but he certainly left his mark of love and beauty on the world and in the lives of many people, including the St. Louis Jesuits. Donald-David's nickname was "Grace;" his life and his spirit continue in the artwork that graces the covers of the St. Louis Jesuits' recordings.

Artist Donald-David Fehrenbach, 1949-1998

It seems clear that the command of Jesus had one concern — do what you do best and do it for Me and Mine. ...Ignatius saw room in his company for men of all abilities and skills in the realization of Christ's kingdom. ...Me? I'm a painter, striving to be an artist. I paint; what and who I am, I paint.... As for Christian art, well, I am a Christian, and since art is self-revelation, my art must be Christian. If it is not, it is because I am not...my painting must project in some, in any way, the message of the Gospel. And that means nudes, bones, portrayals of sacred themes, or whatever, they must rise out of the conviction deep within me that Jesus is Lord to the glory of God the Father...when I have recognized my own small but unique role in the unfolding of the Kingdom, then shall I become an artist.

Donald-David Fehrenbach

When we began looking for artwork for our new anniversary collection, *Morning Light*, we were lucky to find a friend of Donald-David's who owned several of his paintings. Judy Furlong graciously allowed us to use one of these for the cover of the music book and compact disc. For us, Donald-David's work had always communicated, in visual form, the humble prayerfulness we hoped our music could convey through sound. We are thrilled and so grateful to have the beauty of his art on our cover. Nothing else would have seemed appropriate.

Dan Schutte

NEITHER SILVER NOR GOLD

"I have neither silver nor gold, but what I have I will give you."

Liturgical Music from St. Louis Jesuits

EARTHEN VESSELS

music from St. Louis Jesuits

A DWELLING PLACE

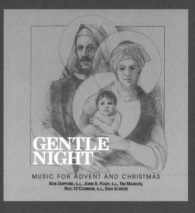

GENTLE NIGHT

MUSIC FOR ADVENT AND CHRISTMAS

Bob Dufford, S.J., John B. Foley, S.J., Tim Manion, Roc O'Connor, S.J., Dan Schutte

WOOD HATH HOPE

Liturgical Music by John Foley, S.J.

Lord of Light

THE STEADFAST LOVE

Liturgical music from St. Louis Jesuits:
Bob Dufford, SJ, John Foley, SJ, Roc O'Connor, SJ, Dan Schutte

LIFT UP YOUR HEARTS

MUSIC FROM THE ST. LOUIS JESUITS ~ VOL. 1

MUSIC FROM THE ST. LOUIS JESUITS ~ VOL 3

LET HEAVEN REJOICE

MAY WE PRAISE YOU

MUSIC FROM THE ST. LOUIS JESUITS ~ VOL. 2

LOVER OF US ALL

LITURGICAL MUSIC BY DAN SCHUTTE

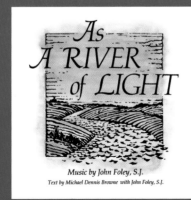

As A RIVER of LIGHT

Music by John Foley, S.J.
Text by Michael Dennis Browne with John Foley, S.J.

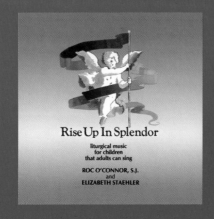

Rise Up In Splendor

liturgical music
for children
that adults can sing

ROC O'CONNOR, S.J.
and
ELIZABETH STAEHLER

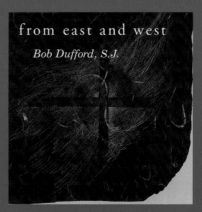

from east and west

Bob Dufford, S.J.

LITURGICAL MUSIC BY DAN SCHUTTE

DRAWN BY A DREAM

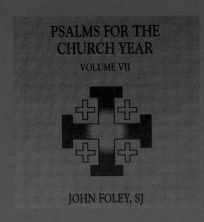

PSALMS FOR THE
CHURCH YEAR
VOLUME VII

JOHN FOLEY, SJ

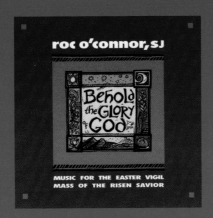

roc o'connor, sj

Behold
the GLORY
of God

MUSIC FOR THE EASTER VIGIL
MASS OF THE RISEN SAVIOR

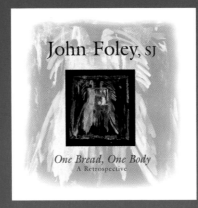

John Foley, SJ

One Bread, One Body
A Retrospective

DAN SCHUTTE
Always & Everywhere

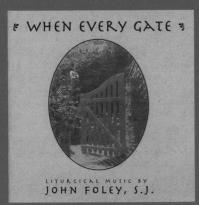

WHEN EVERY GATE

LITURGICAL MUSIC BY
JOHN FOLEY, S.J.

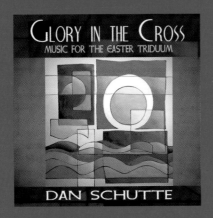

GLORY IN THE CROSS
MUSIC FOR THE EASTER TRIDUUM

DAN SCHUTTE

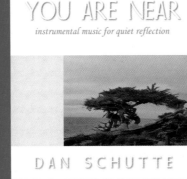

YOU ARE NEAR

instrumental music for quiet reflection

DAN SCHUTTE

LIKE WINTER WAITING

The Advent Story   John Foley, S.J.

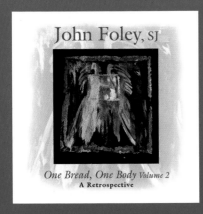

John Foley, SJ

One Bread, One Body Volume 2
A Retrospective

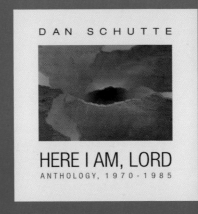

DAN SCHUTTE

HERE I AM, LORD
ANTHOLOGY, 1970-1985

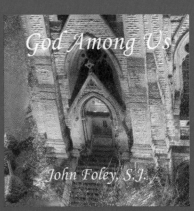

God Among Us

John Foley, S.J.

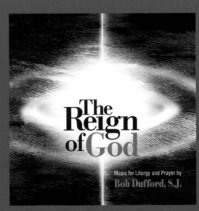

The Reign
of God

Music for Liturgy and Prayer by
Bob Dufford, S.J.

THERE · IS · A · RIVER!
TIM · MANION

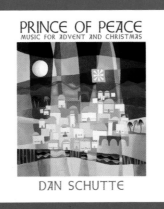

PRINCE OF PEACE
MUSIC FOR ADVENT AND CHRISTMAS

DAN SCHUTTE

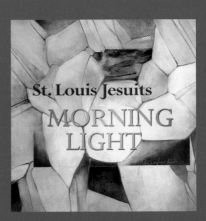

St. Louis Jesuits
MORNING
LIGHT

Berkeley and Beyond

Summer 1974

The response to *Neither Silver Nor Gold* went far beyond the expectations and projections of their publisher, North American Liturgy Resources (NALR) of Cincinnati. Within a few months of its release, there was a need for reprinting the album and songbook.

Their Jesuit superiors were cognizant of the impact this music was having on the life of the church in America. When Bob, Dan, John and Tim asked permission to spend a summer studying music and composing new pieces, their superiors encouraged them to do so and gave them full support. The result was that they, joined now by Roc O'Connor, who had played guitar on their first recording, decided to spend a summer at the Jesuit School of Theology in Berkeley writing and learning.

Berkeley, California

They didn't go to Berkeley imagining that they were going to write music for a new album. Rather, they spent these five weeks composing whatever inspired them and gathering daily to critique and encourage each other's efforts. John Foley had the most formal music training of the five, and he mentored the others in some of the technical aspects of music composition.

The result of the summer was an amazing treasure of new liturgical songs that included "Be Not Afraid," "Though the Mountains May Fall," *Earthen Vessels*, "I Lift Up My Soul" and "Seek the Lord." When it became known to their publisher that they had produced such a large number of new works, Ray Bruno, NALR's publisher, suggested they record a second collection of songs. The Jesuits had not even thought there might be a sequel to *Neither Silver Nor Gold*. God's spirit was leading them down a path they could not have planned.

47

Recording new songs in the Berkeley,
Shalom House, basement

At times, church musicians experience moments that are forever seared into their souls. One of mine took place on a clear, Indian-summer day when students, faculty and staff of the University of Notre Dame poured out onto our main campus. Thousands of us scrambled to celebrate a liturgy filled with hope and comfort in the face of fear and violence. The date was September 11, 2001. At the start of this liturgy, the entire assembly wrapped its vocal cords and hearts around the solace of "Be Not Afraid."

Two generations earlier, working in Vermont, I came across two collections of new ritual music: *Earthen Vessels* and *Neither Silver Nor Gold*. There, in print and vinyl, were names I would return to many times: Dufford, Foley, O'Connor and Schutte. They had begun to create a new musical landscape, one that would help us keep the sung word close to our hearts as we headed out to our daily labors. Their music, in a new but remarkably reverential way, helped us understand that we were, indeed, one body, partaking of one bread.

Some musicians have scoffed at the "tunes" created since the Second Vatican Council. But time and again, when the faithful gathered in times of despair, when families joined in love or when hands were strengthened for sacred work, assemblies reached for the songs of these extraordinary tunesmiths, the Saint Louis Jesuits. For me, whether in 1970 or 2005, it has often been like coming across a precious pearl, a treasure of great value.

Then there is something else — that these men's songs could leave encouraging seeds in my own heart. They urged me to take the chance to write as well, to venture into the labor of wrapping God's word in song. To Bob, John, Roc and Dan, who have become friends and mentors with the passing years, I offer my thanks, together with the thanks of all those who have used these blessed tunes to deepen our faith. Only this have we wanted: to know the Lord, to help us announce the joy of Jesus the Lord. They have shouldered this task with grace, love and memorable songs to keep us true.

Steven C. Warner
Composer
Office of Campus Ministry
University of Notre Dame

When the summer at Berkeley came to a close, the five pooled together the pieces they had written. Roc O'Connor designed a cover for the portfolio of new music. Again they gathered in a basement, the recreation room of the house they were living in for the summer, to record rough versions of their new pieces. In years to come they've referred to these as the Berkeley Basement Tapes. The music composed during this summer would become the backbone of a new recording titled *Earthen Vessels*, which remains the best-selling collection of the St. Louis Jesuits' music.

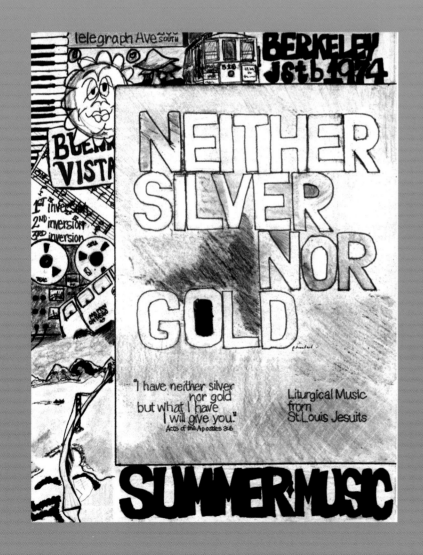

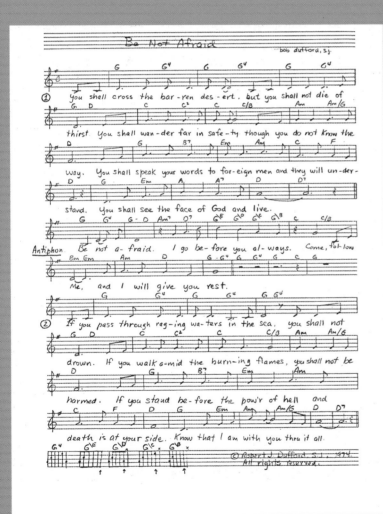

ALL MY DAYS   ALL SHALL BE WELL   ALL THE ENDS OF THE EARTH   ALL

PREPARED   BE NOT AFRAID   BEFORE THE SUN BURNED BRIGHT   BEHOLD

BLESSED BE THE LORD   BLESSINGS ON THE KING   BLEST BE THE LORD   CHILDREN

TO THE WATER   COME WEAL, COME WOE   COME WITH ME INTO THE FI

VESSELS   EMANUEL   EVERY VALLEY   EXULT, YOU JUST ONES   FATHER, MAY

ARE MY GOD   GENTLE NIGHT   GLORY AND PRAISE TO OUR GOD   G

O GOD   HAPPY ARE THE ONES   HEED MY CALL FOR HELP   HERE I AM, L

TO GOD   I FOUND THE TREASURE   IF GOD IS FOR US   IF THE LORD DOES N

WINGS   I LIFT UP MY SOUL   I REJOICED   I WILL SING OF THE LORD   JES

HEAVEN REJOICE   LET THE VALLEYS BE RAISED   LIFT UP YOUR HEARTS   L

MERCY   LORD OF GLORY   MAGNIFICAT   MAY THE ANGELS   MAY WE P

TAKES JOY   MY SON HAS GONE AWAY   NEVER SHALL A SOUL   ONE BRE

LORD   PATIENCE, PEOPLE   PEACE PRAYER   PLAY BEFORE THE LORD

PSALM FIFTY-ONE   PSALM 150   REDEEMER LORD   RESCUE ME FROM MY ENEM

SEEK THE LORD   SEND US YOUR SPIRIT   SERVANT SONG   SHEPHERD, KIND

THE LORD   SING TO THE MOUNTAINS   A SONG OF HOPE   SONGS O

SINGING   THE BEATITUDES   THE BEAUTIFUL MOTHER   THE CHRIST OF GOD   TH

IS MY SHEPHERD   THE PEOPLE THAT WALK IN DARKNESS   THE SPARROW FIND

THE DAY   THOUGH THE MOUNTAINS MAY FALL   TO HIS ANGELS   TO THEE B

ME   VALLEYS OF GREEN   WAKE FROM YOUR SLEEP   WITH DRUMS AND DANC

HEAR IN THE DARK   WINTER COLD NIGHT   WITH MERRY DANCING   WOOD HAT

gs Have Their Time Answer When I Call Awake, Arise A Banquet Is
Lamb Of God Behold The Wood Bless Our God Blessed Are You
n Joyfully CITY OF GOD Come To Me All Who Are Weary Come
Deliver Us, O God Of Israel Doxology Dwelling Place Earthen
y All Be One Father, Mercy Flowers Still Grow There FOR YOU
to God Glory to God God Is Love God's Poor Ones Guide Me,
Holy How Glorious Your Name How Good It Is To Give Thanks
uild In Praise Of His Name In The Morning In The Shadow Of Your
The Lord Just Begun Lamb of God Let All Who Fear The Lord Let
A Shepherd Like Cedars Like The Deer Look Toward Me Lord, Have
You Mighty Lord Mountains And Hills My People My Spirit
ONE BODY Only In God Only This I Want Our Help Is From The
se God Praise The Lord, My Soul Praise To You, Lord Jesus Christ
Return To Your People, O Lord Rise Up, Jerusalem Save Us, O Lord
Holy Sing A New Song Sing All The Earth Sing Of Him Sing To
e Angels Son Of David Take, Lord, Receive A Time Will Come For
RY OF THE POOR The Lord Is Come The Lord Is My Light The Lord
Home The Steadfast Love THIS ALONE This Is My Body This Is
lory Forever To You, I Lift Up My Soul Trust In The Lord Turn To
Who Are We, O Lord Who Has Known Why, O Lord What You
ope Worthy Is The Lamb Yahweh, The Faithful One YOU ARE NEAR

Summer 1975

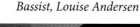
First time recording in a studio

Bassist, Louise Andersen

North American Liturgy Resources can be really proud of this newest work of the St. Louis Jesuits. It is a landmark publication in so many respects. The design and layout of the book are clear and pleasing to the eye. The engraving and editing are probably the best in NALR's history. The performance notes — suggested strums, picking patterns, chord diagrams and even a few theological notes — are unheard of in folk-style publications. And, the music is the finest in this style to be made available to this date.

The collection of twelve pieces, all based on scriptural texts, is a well-rounded sampling of styles: "Praise the Lord, My Soul" and "If God Is for Us," mildly folk-rock; "My Son Has Gone Away," a beautiful solo piece; "Be Not Afraid," a moving solo/choral/congregation piece, and "Though the Mountains May Fall," a vigorous piece.

Earthen Vessels

Jesuits outside recording studio with pianist, Ralph Caccioppo

John, Dan and Bob listen intensely to new tracks

The recording is well done and the string arrangements by John Pell are noteworthy. Even though these are string parts the ranges seem negotiable for other descanting instruments as well. Some of the songs have SATB choir parts but an editorial note is needed here. The altos and tenors sing the melody, the sopranos sing a descant and the basses have their part. This is basically three-part writing and therefore could be easily sung by SSA or TTB choirs.

Parish guitar groups should purchase this fine collection simply from an educational standpoint. Groups that can perform all these pieces could play almost anything. They will also add good new compositions to their repertoire.

— **Review of *Earthen Vessels* published in *Celebration* magazine**

Dan Schutte and Bob Dufford

Tim Manion on banjo

Bob Dufford

Studio photos during recording of Earthen Vessels

I am now in the third week of withdrawal and today is the first day I have awakened without a hangover. Perhaps the dawn is shining forth. As I prayed this morning out of the Bible, I felt maybe God heard me.

I haven't prayed for so long I was fearful. As I listened to *Neither Silver Nor Gold* by the St. Louis Jesuits, I am heartened to step forward and believe in God and in myself. "Come unto me all who are weary and find rest for your soul." In a calmer state now I plead forgiveness for my actions of the past, especially while on drugs. I, in honesty, admit that drugs closed my world. False visions of glory of entering the kingdom of doing good for all came in torrents while on drugs. But freedom is a new high. "Sing a new song unto the Lord. Let your song be sung from mountains high."

— **Anonymous letter, 1976**

Roc O'Connor   *John Foley*

57

Dear Dan,

Today I received from Ray a copy of Earthen Vessels — & while I'm still being "carried" by it I wanted to shoot you note of thanks. Your songs do something very important to me & for me inside. The collection, the production, all that went into it, in my mind stands as the best "thing" I've heard & experienced in all contemporary religious music. It knocks me completely out, I love it, and I feel real good & proud to belong to the same publisher, same universe, same Christian family as you do.

When I think of all the years of being with people who are wrestling with "folk & choirs & "folk choirs" — which has mostly been a euphemism up to now — it'll be a great thing to say — there is music for folk choirs

Anyway, I'm excited about what you all have done. It's some kind of landmark addition to the vocabulary — the album is beautifully infectious — I hum the tunes all day — the scriptures are opened a little further —

just thanks for being who you are,

Joe Wise

P.S. I love it!

3204 LENCOTT DRIVE
LOUISVILLE, KY. 40216

Letter from composer Joe Wise, 1975

Recording Earthen Vessels *in Counterpoint Studio, Cincinnati, Ohio*

*W*hen I reflect upon the work, gift, and contributions that John, Dan, Bob, Roc and Tim have made in liturgical music and for the liturgical reform, I think of so many things: their probing of the Scriptures and providing a voice for a celebrating church aching to sing them; the gift of the many melodies that have continued to sing and pray well after so many years; the witness of their collaboration, brotherhood and friendship; their principle and insistence that music for the liturgy must be prayer, not sacred entertainment; for bridging the gap and renewing the presence and role of the choir in the midst of contemporary composition; for paving the way for so many composers to find a method and approach to writing for the liturgy; and two things that stand out for me in the strongest way — their personal and pastoral integrity, and their common love of the song of the assembly.

I was humbled and honored to be one of the featured soloists on their recording *The Steadfast Love* back in 1985, and have had the pleasure of their friendship, and of working with John and Dan in particular in many settings over the years. I can say without hesitation, that I would not be able to do what I do now both as a liturgical composer and as a minister of the Gospel if not for their groundbreaking work, their creative spirit, their support, and their tremendous generosity and acceptance of their call. All ministry is a call to show who Jesus Christ is, and the St. Louis Jesuits have done just that — in surrendering themselves to become a true vessel of making Christ known to a singing and praying Church.

David Haas
Liturgical Composer
Director, The Emmaus Center for Music, Prayer and Ministry
Eagan, Minnesota

The first St. Louis Jesuit public appearance at a conference in Cincinnati, Ohio, July, 1975

Over the years, the St. Louis Jesuits were hesitant to give concerts. They understood people's desire to hear the music performed by the creators. Their hesitancy arose, however, from a realization that the music they wrote was intended for people to pray with, most often in a liturgical setting. It was never intended to be "performed" as entertainment.

When asked to give a concert, they would often suggest ways in which the music might be presented within the context of a communal prayer event. In their early years they were often presenters at the biennial National Pastoral Musicians' convention. At the first NPM convention in Scranton, Pennsylvania in 1976 they sang at one of four Masses. The convention organizers were not prepared for the response. There was barely room to move in the large gathering space chosen for the Mass. The Communion rite took so long that the Jesuits had to spontaneously lead two additional songs while people received Communion.

In my ongoing journey of conversion, I returned to the church after twenty years in 1986. The church seemed familiar, yet different. One wonderful difference was that people were singing, singing whole-heartedly in scripturally based prayer that was friendly to the untrained voice. I joined in and can't imagine leaving. The music of the St. Louis Jesuits continues to be a part of my conversion. St. Ignatius must be very proud of them.

Finding time to pray is a challenge in our over-extended lives. Listening to the music of the St. Louis Jesuits provides a sacred space of worship and reflection. Their songs have touched my heart and brought me closer to the spirit of God, alive in us all.

Hon. Joanne C. Parrilli
Associate Justice
California Court of Appeals
San Francisco, California

Meeting the members of the St. Louis Jesuits changed my feelings toward the church. For almost twenty years, I worked with each of them individually. They each had a different role within the group. Over the years, I traveled to Toronto, Seattle and other locations to meet with John Foley to discuss ongoing projects. One time, I was invited to stay at the Jesuit house where he was living, and I remember that visit in particular with great gratitude. It was during these few days that the church ceased to be a remote entity, filled with shadows, and it became flesh and blood, a truly living presence.

The greatest influence of my friendship with all four of these extraordinary composers was the eventual exorcism of the soul-deep impression of the church I developed as a child. Growing up in a conservative, joyless, rules-above-all-else grade school had turned me off. The church had changed for the better over the years, but my negative impression remained until I met the dedicated St. Louis Jesuits. They also changed the world of all who celebrated with the music they composed.

David Serey
Serey-Jones Marketing Communications Studio
former Executive Vice President of Epoch/NALR

I took my first job in a Roman Catholic parish in suburban Minneapolis in the summer of 1974. The Franciscan friar I was replacing gave me a good introduction to the Roman post-Vatican II liturgy. He then said, "You might want to listen to this new recording. It might be helpful."

The recording was *Neither Silver Nor Gold*. It was a watershed moment for me in my understanding of the role music can play in embedding Scripture in the hearts of believers. From that date until I was published six years later, my writing was profoundly influenced by that recording and by the many recordings that followed.

The St. Louis Jesuits' collaborations and faithful creations have been a deep and abiding gift to Christians of many denominations. I pray that this reunion will continue to be a reflection of the Spirit's gift to us all.

Marty Haugen
Composer/Liturgical Musician/Author

I would like to share a story about how the music of the St. Louis Jesuits impacted the prayer life of one community. Though I was familiar with the compositions of the St. Louis Jesuits, my first parish job was in the summer of 1982. It was the feast of Corpus Christi. The pastor said, "The people do not like to sing during Communion, so don't bother with them. Just play the organ." I thought I would do an appropriate song, so I sang "One Bread, One Body." After Mass, I was deluged with requests on when they could sing that song. They had never heard Scripture set to song before, and they were moved by the music. It set that community on fire with a love of sung liturgy. That was the start of eight wonderful years of teaching the music of the St. Louis Jesuits to a small suburban parish in the Chicago area.

Mary Prete
General Manager
World Library Publications

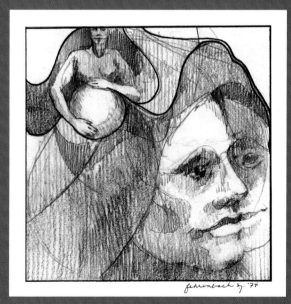

Drawings by Donald-David Fehrenbach

Summer 1976

Bob Dufford rehearsing choir for recording

Dan with NALR producer, Erich Sylvester

During their months apart, they each wrote songs for those who gathered to worship in their communities: the College Church in St. Louis, Holy Rosary and St. Francis Missions in South Dakota, and St. John's Church in Omaha. As they'd write new pieces, they used them almost immediately for liturgy, giving them a chance to access what worked and what needed to be adjusted.

Dwelling Place

Dan Schutte and John Foley　　　*John Foley and Tim Manion*

When you have five composers all writing music during the year, it doesn't take long to compile a significant number of pieces. Their publisher, North American Liturgy Resources, was pleased with the sales of their previous two albums and encouraged them to gather again in Cincinnati to record their new music. Their Jesuit superiors gladly gave permission for them to continue their ministry.

Summer 1976

John Foley with arranger, John Pell

Bassist, Louise Andersen

Tim Manion

Dwelling Place

John Foley directing choir during recording   *String players*

Ray Bruno

As president and founder of North American Liturgy Resources, Ray Bruno was a man of great vision. He had the foresight and instinct to know that the music of the St. Louis Jesuits was something special and initiated the first contact with the Jesuit composers. Rarely does it happen that a publisher comes knocking at a composer's door to ask if they might be interested in having their music published. Ray saw the possibilities not only for the Jesuit music, but of many budding Catholic composers and built NALR into a thriving publishing house. In his final years, he sold the company to Oregon Catholic Press. Ray Bruno died in 1996.

I fondly remember the numerous occasions that I walked into my parents' living room and found five guys sitting on the floor making great music. They were strumming guitars and singing a brand of music I had never heard before at a Sunday Mass.

In the wake of Vatican II, my father, Ray Bruno, started a music publishing company. In the process, he stumbled upon five St. Louis seminarians he believed could "get the church singing again." My father was a visionary, and he surrounded himself with others who shared his passion for returning the language of prayer to the community. Bob, Dan, John, Roc and Tim quickly became fixtures in our home, our ministry and our hearts. During those early days, we were a family in every sense of the word. I remember celebrating Christmas in June during the recording of *Gentle Night*. We were surrounded by gifts and a recording-studio Christmas tree.

North American Liturgy Resources (NALR) began publishing music that was both a pleasure to sing and liturgically based. The group was named by my father when he needed a name for the cover of their first collection, *Neither Silver Nor Gold*. The songs of this first project married contemporary folk melodies with scriptural lyrics and, in the process, set a future course for liturgical music. It was "usable" music, and even I realized its power when I brought my guitar to school Mass to test songs from the *Earthen Vessels* collection.

Thirty years later, I had the pleasure of joining the Saint Louis Jesuits in the studio for the recording of *Morning Light*. All of us were a little older, but the faith, spirit and great music remained unchanged. I felt the familiar warmth of Dan's embrace when I entered the room and smiled as John napped on the floor, his head resting on his guitar case. I quickly remembered that look of concentration on Roc's face as he listened to the playbacks, and I laughed at the ability of Tim and Bob to add the silly element to a serious moment.

I now have no doubt that the Saint Louis Jesuits were largely responsible for the successes of NALR and our many artists. For this we have much to celebrate and be grateful for.

Bruce R. Bruno
Trade and International Sales, Oregon Catholic Press
Son of Ray Bruno, Founder and President of North American Liturgy Resources

Summer 1977

Throughout the years composing for liturgy, each of the St. Louis Jesuits had opportunities to write music for the season of Advent and Christmas. Upon completing their *Dwelling Place* recording the previous summer, the five began to consider doing a seasonal collection that would include these yet unpublished pieces.

When they pooled together the songs from previous years, they found they already had nearly enough for another collection of songs. They realized they needed some upbeat, fast-tempo pieces that would be in contrast to their slower, more contemplative songs. Between the summer of 1976 and the next year, each composed new pieces to create a more balanced collection.

In the summer of 1977, they gathered in Phoenix to record a new collection of music for Advent and Christmas, *Gentle Night*. Each composer had grown up in climates where the Christmas season meant cold and snow and ice. Here they were in Phoenix! It was the hottest time of the year, and they were recording an album of Christmas music. To help get them in the mood to record, someone brought several strings of Christmas lights to adorn the recording studio. The songs that resulted from these days in Phoenix are still some of their most beloved and treasured works. That year, the St. Louis Jesuits celebrated Christmas in the desert!

Gentle Night

What I meant to say...is that, of all the ways to get through which I found to sustain me during an excruciatingly difficult period of my life, the most consoling by far was *Gentle Night*. The hours I spent playing the recording, thanks in part to weeks of mandatory home leave decreed jointly by the doctors and the firm, were countless. I got well spiritually by listening to *Gentle Night*.

I can't begin to tell you how rich and magical I found that recording. I can assure you that it has both beauty and power. It will drive anyone...with an honest curiosity about the mystery and the miracle of Christmas past contemplation, into wonder and belief. It is more than music and prayer. It is testimony of astonishing power.

— **Excerpt from a letter to John Foley in November, 1977**

Photos taken in Omaha, Nebraska, winter 1977

My earliest memories of the music of the St. Louis Jesuits were in 1977. Just out of college, I was employed in a parish. I asked for help from folks who did music in area churches. They handed me *Neither Silver Nor Gold* and *Earthen Vessels*. This was my first exposure to contemporary liturgical music that was scriptural, harmonically interesting for the style and produced with strings, wood-winds and a choir. I felt it was a legitimate attempt at writing quality music that ultimately got the job done. Their music fit the liturgy and was singable.

Later that year, I attended the first NPM convention in Scranton and spoke with John Foley and Dan Schutte about how meaningful their music was in my life, both personally and professionally. It was their music that inspired me to pursue a similar path. I have been honored to produce recordings of their individual projects, and I continue to be blessed by their contribution to the work of the Gospel and the sung praise in the liturgy.

Tom Kendzia
Composer
Director of Music, Christ the King Parish in Kingston, RI

Summer 1980

After the release of *Gentle Night*, the group decided to take the next summer off from their yearly schedule of recording. John Foley, who had always been the most prolific of the group, took this opportunity to produce a collection of his own music. Enlisting the help of the others in the group, John proceeded with the recording of his collection of eleven new pieces in a collection titled *Wood Hath Hope*. During the spring of 1978, members of the group visited the Phoenix studio to add their voices and instrumental ability to the recording.

It would be two years before the composers gathered again to record as a group. In the summer of 1980, they returned to St. Louis to record another collection of liturgical music. With several years having elapsed since their last recording, there was a wealth of new music to choose from.

In the end, they settled on eleven of their best songs, including "City of God," "Jesus the Lord," "Lift Up Your Hearts" and "Here I Am, Lord," to fill out the collection *Lord of Light*. Worship communities received the new music with great enthusiasm. In time, this collection proved to be one of their most popular, second only to *Earthen Vessels*.

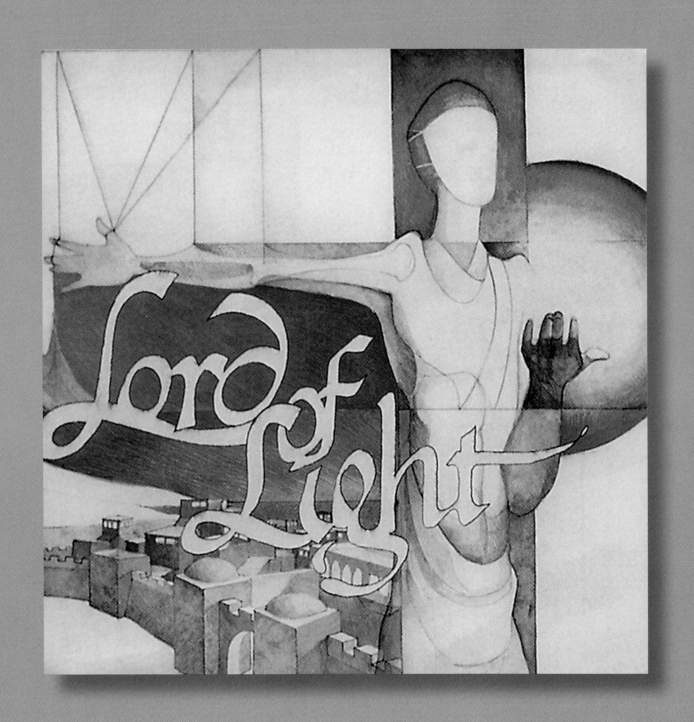

1980–1983 Seattle, Washington

In early 1980, the five composers were scattered across the world. Bob Dufford was teaching at Creighton Preparatory, a school for boys run by the Jesuits in Omaha, Nebraska. Roc O'Connor and Dan Schutte were completing their theological studies in Berkeley, California. Tim Manion lived in St. Louis, Missouri, the homeland of their musical birth, and John Foley was pursuing further compositional study in London, England. It was a turning point in their lives as they wondered where the musical journey might take them.

It's important to remember that this was in the days prior to e-mail messaging, so the process of communication was slow. Over a period of months, the idea emerged that, if there was ever a time when they might devote their lives to music, this was it. God seemed to open a door to the possibility for Bob, Dan, Roc and Tim to pursue more formal studies in music to complement their considerable experience and informal learning. John was beginning work on a monumental oratorio called *Book of Glory*, and he needed concentrated time to work on this project.

After some coaxing, Jesuit Father Kevin Waters, the director of the fine arts program at Seattle University and well-established composer in his own right, agreed to fashion a program of study flexible enough to meet their needs. In practice, Kevin became their private mentor and musical instructor for the next several years.

St. Louis Jesuits with their music mentor, Fr. Kevin Waters, S.J. Seattle, Washington 1981

ST. LOUIS JESUITS: A TOUCH OF "CLASS" AT SEATTLE UNIVERSITY

Four members of one of the most prominent groups of liturgical musicians in the country — the St. Louis Jesuits — are spending this year studying in the university's Fine Arts Department. One of the main reasons the group is at the university is to study compositional technique under Fr. (Kevin) Waters. Although all members grew up with music and have extensive experience, much of their training has been informal.

Last year the St. Louis Jesuits were recipients of a special award from Cashbox magazine, a respected music trade journal, for "significant and lasting contribution to gospel music over the last twenty years." Other recipients of the award included Bob Dylan, Mahalia Jackson, Elvis Presley, Tennessee Ernie Ford and Pat Boone. Last spring, the St. Louis Jesuits received additional recognition — honorary doctorates from the University of Scranton.

— **Excerpt from Seattle University *Sun*, January 31, 1981 issue, article by Mark Burnett**

*I*n 1980, I received a phone call from John Foley asking me if I would be interested in offering a year-long workshop in compositional technique to some members of the St. Louis Jesuits. John had already completed formal programs in theory and composition and felt it would increase the efficiency of the group if everyone had a similar background. My imagination and basic interest went into high gear over the possibility of exploring music with highly talented composers who had already produced six albums and were awaiting the production of a seventh.

At the end of my own doctoral studies in composition, I developed a keen desire to uncover a method of teaching people to compose. In fact, I went to Europe after my formal studies to converse with a number of composers including Godfredo Petrassi, Olivier Messiaen and Elliot Carter (who was then teaching at the American Academy in Rome) to elicit their acquired wisdom about this. I also spent several months studying with Bruno Bartolozzi, who was a leader in the Italian avant-garde movement of composition. Now I had an opportunity to put what I knew and planned to develop further into a living workshop.

An instructor learns early that one can only teach a few things to all one's students, whether they are gifted or ordinary. One will always be on the outside and able to only "proofread" what was written and offer tips on fundamental techniques. I vividly recall that I intended that Bob, Dan, Roc and Tim write a lot of exercises to loosen up their compositional joints. They resisted. They were reluctant to waste time and wanted to get right down to writing a finished product. Very few genuine exercises ever got on paper during the time the group spent with me, but a few notable compositions emerged and I believe were eventually performed, published and recorded.

My responsibility in changing the dynamics of the St. Louis Jesuits haunted me in 1980. Would this group, which had a unified style and approach to music, be altered radically by the workshop? Would the individuality of each composer come to the fore in such a way that the distinctive style of the group began to fade or even disappear?

I do not believe that I can answer those questions now. But perhaps the questions have changed or, perhaps they no longer matter.

Kevin Waters, S.J.
Professor of Music
Gonzaga University

After completing his second year of music study in Seattle, Dan Schutte moved to Milwaukee to work at Marquette University. The others remained in Seattle but, during that year, Tim Manion confided that he no longer wanted to write and record liturgical music. It seemed the group's time of collaboration was perhaps ending.

After many hours of discussion and trying to discern the movement of God's spirit in their lives, the group decided it was time to follow individual paths. They didn't say they would never record together again, but agreed it was time for a separation.

Before they did this, and even without Tim's presence, they decided to do one last recording together. During their years of study and work in Seattle, each of them had created new pieces. When they pooled their compositions, they realized they had enough music for several albums. They chose to record a new collection of twenty-two pieces, *The Steadfast Love*. This would be their final collective work.

Then and Now

Bob Dufford, S.J.

I used to go to Mass almost daily when I was younger. Often the girls wouldn't show up, so I'd go back there and sing. That continued into high school. I'd mow the lawn and sing at the top of my voice, making up songs or singing songs I knew. I figured nobody could hear me.

"...the music...rich and full...honored the spectrum of human feelings."

Joe Wise
Composer and Artist

I remember beginning to hear the music of Bob, Dan, John, Roc and Tim. It was rich and full. For me, it honored

the spectrum of human feelings. It was especially welcome with so many worship and prayer elements having served

their lives, while at the same time, affirming that which is mystical. It was a sophisticated addition to a burgeoning

contemporary faith-and-worship song phenomenon.

I always felt honored to share a stage with them. I have a fond m emory of working with Bob and Roc at a Canadian

liturgical gathering. The planning sessions for this event included tenderness and hilarity in equal measure.

It is hard to imagine how poor the English-speaking Christians' song vocabulary would be without the gifts the

St. Louis Jesuits brought so generously to the table. — J.W.

How did you get interested in music?

My dad was very interested in music. He had a little band, a quartet that used to play all around the Midwest. It was a great little group with a bass, guitar and harmonica. He loved music, played the piano and harmonica and sang. I had piano lessons in second grade for about six weeks, but I couldn't stand them. I couldn't get it, and it drove me nuts. I never learned to play an instrument until I was studying philosophy in college.

When I started going to Mass around sixth grade, I started singing in choirs and learned all the chants. I used to go to Mass almost daily when I was younger. Often the girls wouldn't show up, so I'd go back there and sing. That continued into high school. I'd mow the lawn and sing at the top of my voice, making up songs or singing songs I knew. I figured nobody could hear me. A lot of it was connected with the liturgy.

I loved Broadway musicals. My folks had a high-fidelity set. We'd play records and listen to My Fair Lady and Tchaikovsky. I would imagine conducting the orchestra. When nobody was home, I'd turn up the volume and conduct. It continued when I entered the Jesuits. The changes in the liturgy were happening just as I was entering the juniorate. I directed the choir and sang in the choir all the time. I learned a few things about music from Barney Portz.

What were your influences?

I was influenced by Broadway musicals: Rodgers and Hammerstein, Lerner and Lowe, Oklahoma, My Fair Lady, Camelot and Oliver. I was also influenced by classical music: Tchaikovsky, Bach, Beethoven and Handel. When I got into the novitiate, three or four of us, on the first Christmas, listened to the complete Messiah. We did it once a year. I just felt in love with Handel. A lot of the early songs I did were influenced by him. For example, in "Every Valley," Handel's "He shall feed his flock, like a shepherd" becomes "Like a shepherd, he feeds his flock." I just wanted people to listen to Handel, and I thought this was one way to do it. I knew pop music, but I wasn't trying to imitate it.

What was it like hitting it big?

I was sitting in my room, working on this little chord pattern, and I was singing a melody against it. This was in St. Louis, about nine months after I had gotten a guitar. I had just learned to play a couple months before that. I had just started to notate this little song when a guy from New York Province came in and said, "What are you doing?" He asked me to sing the song, so I did. Then he said, "We gotta use that for Good Friday." I said, "What?" I had no idea it was going to touch other people. I just wrote music for myself. When I found out other people liked it, I was amazed.

When I was in tertianship, there were four of us, and two of us went out to the Indian missions. I thought, "This will be good. I can get away from the celebrity bit for a while, and nobody is going to know who the St. Louis Jesuits are on the missions." I ended up doing four workshops while I was out there. My spiritual director told me, "Maybe what you learned is that this is part of your life, and you have to deal with it." It's not always a big thing, it's just not always a plus. The hard part has been learning to use it and also to let go of it so I don't start thinking of it as something people owe me.

In the heyday, the mid-1970s through 1995, I was doing fifteen to twenty-five workshops a year around the United States and Canada. I made it to all but seven states in the US. Roc and I also did workshops in Australia. It's mind boggling that people would pay money to have us fly here and there. I learned a lot about liturgy by trying to put words around it. I read a lot about liturgy and I learned about it from doing it. When I'd be in a workshop and trying to explain things to people, I could see their eyes kind of glaze over. The fact that I was standing in front of them was far more important than anything I was trying to say. It was as though this was working against my ministry. I found I had to use humor to cut through, to remind people we put our pants on one leg at a time, too, and that it just so happened that we knew how to help people sing.

What happened after *Lord of Light*? How did you guys decide to go in different directions?

Our studies were over and our lives changed. We had individual ministries and that pulled people apart. When we were all teaching in a school, we had summers available. Some of us didn't even have that. It was not because we didn't like each other. The easiest of all the albums to make was The Steadfast Love because we had grown together and learned to appreciate each other, to love each other. Lord of Light was very painful and very hard. We were just starting to live together. We had grown to care for each of the guys in a very different way than before. After that, we were all in different places. It was never a conscious decision not to do something together, it just happened.

What has been your path since?

I still did a lot of workshops. I was at Creighton University for eleven years. A lot of the focus was on working with liturgy and understanding liturgy, getting it to work and talking with people about it. I also did a lot of computer work. The personal computer had begun by then, and it was a major interest of mine. I also directed many retreats as I'd always had an interest in spirituality. My master's degree is in ascetical/mystical theology (which means spirituality). The first thing I did, after I got ordained, was direct a thirty-day retreat. That's how I learned to do the Spiritual Exercises myself. I've loved the Exercises since the first time I made them.

Also, I love talking to people about Jesus. At Creighton, after a practice, somebody would want to go out for a burger or pizza. We'd go and talk about life. One woman used to sing with Rodgers and Hammerstein in New York, and she knew Richard Rodgers. She said that I reminded her of him. She just wanted to talk about all that. I love talking to people about God and freeing them from images of God that they seem to get trapped in. That's what the music does, too. If people are trapped by distorted images of God, the music can provide new images so they can see God is much more than they thought, something of delight and not fear. The retreat work I do is a part of that, as are preaching, conversations and music. They all free people from distorted images of God.

What's the state of liturgical music today? What are its strengths and needs?

First of all, liturgical music is not monolithic. It's not one thing; it's all over the place. Because it's going in so many different directions at once, you can't say anything about it all together. There are several trends. One trend is away from what we've done into what feels to be more distancing music. They seem to be songs that don't touch the heart; they are songs that are correct and are approved. Some are songs that don't ask too much of me, that let me remain distant and in the pew. That saddens me because it seems it will eventually distance us from God.

There's concern about the proper, official texts, about the importance of them meeting certain guidelines. I'm not totally convinced that is what people want. We have people come to the Oshkosh retreat house where I now work. It's like an oasis for them, and they tell us they don't want to go to Mass, so they come up here for solace.

There are new publishing emphases on music, not just for liturgy but for prayer and contemplation. I think that's wonderful; that's exactly the decision I've made. Haydn, Handel and Beethoven would write Masses, but suddenly there were all these strictures set down prohibiting their use so, instead of writing Masses, they wrote oratorios and music for prayer services. They would be held in the churches but not be centered on liturgy. I'm seeing a similar movement going on in contemporary society. Because one door shuts, we'll do something else.

What are your images of God?

I have all kinds of images of God. Take a song, such as "Like A Shepherd." The refrain is very calm. To me, that provides a soft and quiet image, symbolizing the gentleness of God. Then there's a strong sound and the song picks up tempo. That's the strength of God. The two qualities are blended seamlessly in God. People need to see that both are there.

The song "Worthy is the Lamb" is a big, gigantic major scale piece. Its text is from Revelation. There's a big Roman army coming in; the Lord is coming; watch for majesty, power, glory and strength! Then it suddenly goes into 3/4 time and into a minor key. It's kind of mysterious and weird. For me, the book of Revelation is like that. There is one side of it that is big and gigantic in power; a two-edged sword is coming out and the iron rod will beat up the nations. You also have a sense of wonder and amazement going right alongside of it. Both are part of the image of God for me. He is power and majesty, something transcendent, the center of all that is and simultaneously, he is the one who loves and knows intimate details about us. He's a parent who delights in seeing the child grow. Once the child starts using freedom, mistakes will be made, but wonderful things also start to happen. I could say God is like a parent, but that alone is not going to do it for many people. For me, to say God is father, had to come through prayer. I wasn't very close to my own father. I am now, but not then. Many of my images of father came from members of the Society of Jesus: Joe Sheehan, S.J., Bob Purcell, S.J. and Len Waters, S.J.

That is why I do music. I strive to come up with images of God, like God as a parent calling the son home. In "Come Home," the child longs for home, and what he's been trying to substitute for home just isn't going to work. The wrong path is going to end pretty soon; when it does, he's invited to come home. When things run out, come back to me, God invites. Let go of that which dulls your heart. Images for me are not just visual. They tend to be musical, images of sound.

What has the St. Louis Jesuit adventure been like for you?

It has certainly been an adventure. In my early years, I was focused on teaching philosophy and math. Somewhere in my 30s, I figured there were others who could do that but not as many who were creating music for people at prayer. Our music is not aimed at explaining things of faith but at creating a thing that God might use to touch human hearts.

When I explain something, I attempt a short-range control of another's thought process in hopes that the other may get the same idea I had. With song, I let go of all that control. A new song is not an idea but a thing, something that never existed before. A song is more like a child who has a life separate from mine. I try to give it a good start, one that helps it be heard at its best, but the time arrives when the song must make its way into the world on its own. Sometimes it comes home to touch me in ways I never planned.

One of the gifts of this adventure has been learning how liturgy, done well, can influence people. I would not have been involved in liturgy if not for this work with the St. Louis Jesuits. Music, like poetry and drama, allows the past to pile up into the present. All the time spent on words and images, vowel sounds and meaning, melody, chords and instrumentation is folded into a few short minutes, creating a vehicle for God to touch lives.

Another gift has been getting to know other men — Jesuit brothers, musicians and composers — who are doing the same thing. We all have a similar way of wanting to do this. We have been stretched and challenged. There are chord progressions, strum patterns and instrumentations I would never have tried had it not been my work with John, Roc and Dan.

John Foley, S.J.

Some Jesuits at Regis College ran classical music appreciation classes. They showed us what went on in each classical piece. I had never known any of this. I used to jump over a wall in a quonset hut building to get to the piano at night. I'd make up classical pieces and sonatas, because that's what I was learning in the classical music classes.

"As my former students, they have gone beyond their teacher."

James Empereur, S.J.
Vicar and Liturgist at San Fernando Cathedral
San Antonio, Texas

In so many ways the St. Louis Jesuits embody those
qualities that I have most valued in the celebration of the
liturgy: a biblical freshness, an engaging musicality, and
an artful liturgical sensibility. As my former students,
they have gone beyond their teacher. As companions in
many liturgies in the past, they have bequeathed to me
some of my richest memories. They really did sing a new
church into being. — J.E.

What did you want to be when you grew up?

I was a composer from the time I was a little kid. I started piano lessons at about five and, by the time I got out of high school, I was kind of a good classical pianist. I thought of the Jesuits in senior high school in Wichita, Kansas, but I was more interested in romance, and I was still interested in music. I put it aside, and I went to Regis College in Denver. When I started taking philosophy in college, I really wanted to be a philosopher. I had too many things I wanted.

Some Jesuits at Regis ran these classical music appreciation classes. They showed us what went on in each classical piece. I had never known any of this. I had only played them. It made such sense; it made things come together so beautifully. At Regis I used to jump over a wall in a quonset hut building to get to the piano at night. I'd make up these classical pieces and sonatas, because that's what I was learning in the classical music classes. Then I'd make those Jesuits come over and listen to them. They were really responsible for a lot of my desire to go into music. I went to music school at Wichita State the year after I graduated from college, and the Jesuits still seemed pretty good. I did not know anything about the Jesuit novitiate or anything like that; I didn't know anything about discernment. I just sort of asked God, "Which one do you want me to do?" I made God take responsibility for it.

How did you come to start composing music for Masses?

In the novitiate, there was a piano in the basement of the church, but we had to get permission to use it. I could get permission once a month. I'd been practicing the piano six hours a day before I entered and suddenly had next to nothing. I got some other novices to show me chords on the guitar. Just at that time, the guitar started to be allowed in the new liturgy. I thought, "Well, they need music, so let's go." It was a matter of timing that was right. I wanted to be part of a movement that gave Vatican II's call for participation a chance and gave people melodies they could sing and also were sophisticated and had spirituality attached to them, the spirituality of the Mass. I'd write pieces and send them to various publishing companies and get rejection letters. Nearly everything I had in Neither Silver Nor Gold *had been previously rejected, but the music was really successful here in St. Louis, and by that time, Bob, Dan, Roc and Tim were all in the city.*

How exactly did you get connected with the others?

My memory is that I heard their music over at Fusz, and I heard a rumor they were going to write it all down. I said, "Hey, let's gather me and any other Jesuits in St. Louis who have been writing liturgical music, and we'll put out copies of it when people ask for it." My stuff started to get around; Schutte and Dufford got copies of it, and they started writing in their own unique ways. I was doing short refrains, setting those antiphons that are printed in the missal, that are remnants of the chant from ancient days. When he got to St. Louis, Dan started to do longer refrains that had a lot more melodic content. I had based mine on Joseph Gelineau's, in part, but when I heard his, I thought that it really fit the American idiom. That was what Vatican II told us we should use for inculturation purposes. An attractive melody for a refrain helped people remember it and made the spirituality more personal. That's when I started "One Bread, One Body" and other songs with longer refrains.

This guy came to see me, a new publisher, and said, "We're very hungry, and we've heard about your music." When I told him we were planning to self-publish, he offered to be our publisher. We were very uncertain at first; maybe it was excessive naïveté, but we just wanted to have something to give out. I had been interested in publishing, but after having gotten so many rejection letters, thought maybe it wasn't meant to be. Then we decided to do it, and that was the start. We had no idea they'd put out the whole collection and the book Dan had engraved by hand.

How did your music develop as a group?

The people playing guitars those days were younger. We felt if they heard something highly professional, they would say, "We could never do that." It would discourage them instead of encourage them. Before making Earthen Vessels, we went to Cincinnati and looked at a studio with the publisher, and suddenly we got the idea of putting down the basic tracks — piano, guitar, and our voices — as we always did. The younger players could work with that, and then we could add tracks, like strings and oboe, with professionals. That was the way to have the best of both worlds and was the way we recorded Earthen Vessels. No matter what we tried to do

instrumentally, we tried to keep our parts simple. We made each album we put out a little more complicated because we thought we would be teaching the guitar crowd to be better and better. But there wasn't the continuity we thought there would be. There would be people playing guitars for two to three years, and then they'd go to college or go into business and a new crowd would come in, so we gradually professionalized the whole thing and raised the guitar playing standards.

People talk about your work together as capturing the rhythms and speech well.

The ultimate roots are with Fr. Bob Boyle at Regis. I studied Hopkins with him at college. I heard the sprung and metaphorical rhythm, and I just fell in love with it. Working in language from that point on became something I couldn't compromise. It's actually easier to get the rhythms of the language right than to do them wrong. It's like a guy who lays bricks and lays them all crooked. I'm not making any claims that I did it right all the time.

What happened after *Steadfast Love*? What did you do after the split?

After you've been working together for twelve or fourteen years, it's hard to keep doing the same music. People had their own interests. You mature and grow in different directions over that period. It was tough leaving, but I am sure it was the best thing to do. We toasted one another, went our separate ways, and remained friends. I had already studied classical music at the Royal Conservatory of Toronto and in London with Reginald Smith Brindle. I then moved to the novitiate in St. Paul, Minnesota. The novice director, Gene Merz, said, "This will be a great place for you. We'll support you. It's a music city." I was there writing music for five years.

I discovered there that I'm more an extrovert, more a teacher than a scholar. When writing classical music, one has to spend a lot of time alone writing, with paper, pencil and one's mind. I did it, but it made me unhappy. So I asked to do more. I could do the introvert work if I did the extrovert work, too. I went to Berkeley and got a doctorate in liturgical/ascetical theology.

I then went to St. Louis University with the idea of forming a center for liturgy. The Second Vatican Council said we should have centers for liturgy to study liturgy and to teach people how to be part of the liturgy. I took my idea to the university president, and he gave it his support. We tried out many different plans. One was going to parishes and talking about the liturgy, but that didn't reach far enough. We put on prayer services for liturgical ministers in the city. We then started a Web site, liturgy.slu.edu, and that worked. It proved to be a major resource. The Lily Foundation gave a grant to St. Louis University that included support for a liturgical intern program. We place undergrads in parishes for a full year, teach them about the liturgy and send them to workshops. We also run a composers' forum, inviting published liturgical composers. There is a convention each year that is well attended. I teach liturgical theology in the graduate school.

How did you end up getting back together at the NPM convention?

It was the occasion of the retirement of the founder of NPM, Fr. Virgil Funk. Additionally, Oregon Catholic Press planned an event to mark the twenty-fifth anniversary of NPM. There was a small orchestra and Gerard Chiusano served as the very able conductor. Toward the end of the event, the narrator announced, "There are four men that have not sung together since they stopped recording and making music to-gether." He said, "We want to introduce the St. Louis Jesuits!" The audience's reaction was as if the Beatles had just gotten back together. For us, it was shades of the old days, when popular music was more a part of liturgy.

We didn't know until just before the convention that we were going to do it. We had said we were willing, but the publisher hadn't followed up. Then just before the convention, they let us in on the plan. They didn't want anybody to know, prefer-ring it be a surprise. All along, we had never given concerts. We never stood on stage except at an NPM convention. We were writing liturgical music but weren't writing music to be presented on stage. We didn't give concerts; we gave workshops. The events weren't about us; they were about the Mass and the music. The concern for each of us has always been to keep the spotlight on the music.

What are your images of God?

I really love thinking of the Trinity. Much of the music on my new album is Trinitarian. We discover the Trinity by seeing how God has treated us in each of the different covenants. God, the Father, has repeatedly pursued us; we come back and then we go away again. We Christians believe that God said, "Now is the time for a new covenant and the covenant will be the same as the old one. I will be your God and you will be my people, just be faithful, like I am." He decided the only way to get it done was to have a human being come and be faithful to God's covenant. It is a very earthy story instead of something in the sky. Jesus comes back in the resurrection, and says, "I can't stay with you, but I will stay with you by sending you a comforter, a new teacher in your hearts." God is with us always, in the body of Christ. Jesus is with us, in our midst and also sitting at the right hand of the Father. It's the most rewarding image of God that I have. It's like God's embrace is everywhere if we'll accept it.

What has the St. Louis Jesuit adventure been like for you?

There was a surprise waiting at the Jesuit novitiate when I entered at 22: there was no accessible piano. I had played piano since I was six and had studied composition at Wichita State University. Just for fun, I asked a fellow novice to show me some guitar chords. I had already written choral music for choir, organ and individual instruments, but suddenly the guitar-group trend began in the church. I considered whether I could contribute something to that. Since I was a classical musician, I had never dreamed of writing popular church music. The guitar sort of fell into my hands, so to speak.

I began writing in various styles but settled into the type of music that would come to be published ten years later. My most prominent song of that period was "For You Are My God."

I practiced and took all kinds of lessons, including ones at the music school at Washington University in St. Louis. About ten years after I began with the guitar, there came a confluence. All of us Jesuit musicians were stationed in St. Louis for studies. We gathered informally, collected music we each had written and learned from one another. For instance, I had been concentrating on short refrains similar to the ones Joseph Gelineau pioneered, but I noticed that Dan Schutte wrote longer and more lyrical refrains. I composed "Turn to Me" and "One Bread, One Body" as a direct result.

Suddenly, a publisher showed up at the door and wanted to publish our music — all of it. We agreed reluctantly, and the result, surprisingly, became history. The first collection, Neither Silver nor Gold, *to our astonishment, sold widely, even with 63 pieces of liturgical music in it. The next publication,* Earthen Vessels, *became the largest selling liturgical collection ever and, as far as I know, remains so, even to this day.*

God was guiding the St. Louis Jesuits over all these years, amidst the fun and the very hard work it took. Love of liturgy in each of us and our desire to give music to the people was God's initiative. I believe grace was the glue that held us together for so many years.

Tim Manion

In high school, we had this very cool Mass at midnight on Saturday. People went on dates and then came to midnight Mass. I got involved in this little music group that played for that. There wasn't anybody to play bass, and one guy thought he could teach me to play four notes. When we needed a guitar player, I swapped to that. That was my first exposure to that kind of thing.

"...through my exposure to the music of the St. Louis Jesuits that I was led to Catholicism..."

Bobby Fisher

Composer and Musician, Faculty of NPM Guitar School

Some of my earliest experience as a studio musician involved playing mandolin on "What You Hear in the Dark" from the *Earthen Vessels* album and banjo on "Lord of Glory" from *Dwelling Place*. At the time I was a fairly new Christian, but had not yet committed to the Catholic faith.

It was in part through my exposure to the music of the St. Louis Jesuits that I was led to Catholicism and later influenced to become involved in music ministry and liturgical composition. I am blessed that our friendship that began then has continued through the years. Thank you, Dan, John, Bob, Roc, and Tim. —**B.F.**

Where are you from?

I'm from St. Louis. I have one younger, adopted sister, and we grew up in the suburb of St. Louis called Florissant. We grew up in a Catholic — but not fanatically so — family, but St. Louis is a pretty Catholic town. Parish life was school life and sports life and social life.

What did you want to be when you grew up? How did music become a part of your life?

I certainly didn't plan on being a musician! I loved music when I was a kid, but other than the normal kid things, the first thing I really perceived was a solid desire to be a Jesuit. That desire is what took me into the Jesuits in the first place. In high school, we had this very cool Mass at midnight on Saturday. People went on dates and then came to midnight Mass. I got involved in this little music group that played for that. There wasn't anybody to play bass, and one guy thought he could teach me to play four notes. When we needed a guitar player, I swapped to that. That was my first exposure to that kind of thing. I did it long enough that it carried over to the novitiate.

I entered the Jesuits in the fall of 1969. Our novice director used to sit and play piano, singing "A Foggy Day in London Town" and "Danny Boy." His name was Vince O'Flaherty, and he entered the Society after the war. He had done some piano-bar playing before entering the Jesuits. He was very influential on me and on us; he was kind of an artistic guy, and he encouraged the music among us. It was a fortuitous thing to be around his influence at that time.

Who were your musical influences?

As I got older, out of high school and into college, I loved all kinds of folk music and bluegrass. I played bluegrass in a bar after I left the Jesuits. I could get people up and dancing but they'd throw stuff at us, too.

I also liked Motown when I first became aware of that music — the Temptations and such. That was St. Louis dance music. Later on, there were classical influences as music became more a part of my life.

Looking back, what do you remember? What are your impressions?

It seems like I have fifty billion memories. I remember Christmas lights in a recording studio in July in Phoenix so we could do Gentle Night. I remember doing one album, and the other guys had to scatter for the holidays and I was there working on the editing. When I picked up John up at the airport, I said, "There are two pieces of news. First, we're moving right along on the editing. Second, the producer has been arrested and the tapes have been seized!"

My overall feeling is I wouldn't trade it for anything. It was totally formative of who I am. The St. Louis Jesuits remained the center of my life for a number of years after I left. I went with them out to Seattle, got married there and had my son there. It was an absolutely central and formative part of my life that I wouldn't trade for anything. It was good, the time I spent with these really different guys with different takes on life, on everything. Of course, we had times when all I wanted to do was rip out somebody's throat. It was the kind of experience that has that texture. As I look back on it, I know intellectually there were times like that, but I can't really feel it.

We were pretty big frogs in the small pond of Catholic music. It was fun to be recognized and to go to different places, to make a living doing workshops all over the country. I think we did some good work. I think we added to the atmosphere of the church in the country. How many times does one get a chance to have that kind of effect on other people's lives? It was a good run.

What was it like to work together?

I always enjoyed being with all the guys. Mostly it was fun. While some moments were tense, there was also tons of enjoyment from joking around. We had the kind of comradeship that results from time spent together doing something creative. That's why that experience was so formative. I spent a lot of years working at being in relationship with a group of guys, and most people don't get the chance to do that. At Fusz, early on, it was just kind of an extension of something that I had enjoyed in high school. There was just the basic enjoyment of being able to continue to do that in maybe a bigger venue. The major point was that we transitioned from being some Jesuits doing music in St. Louis to being the St. Louis Jesuits. I think the experiences were great and one led really naturally to the other.

For you, what were some of the central moments in the history of the group?

Berkeley in 1974 was central. It was the first time we acknowledged we were trying to do more than work together in this Mass ritual program. We became something else and were recognized as something else.

Each album was important. The experience of creating something like that is so absorbing, from preparation to studio time to working with other musicians and choirs. Each phase of production had its own flavor and probably had to do with the music and where each of us was in life.

For me, the time at the end was important. I decided to move away from living that life of being a part of the group. There were elements of the group that weren't working for me anymore. The biggest element of that was me. Ultimately, my spirituality was changing.

What did you do after leaving the St. Louis Jesuits?

After I left, I was still working at a church in Seattle. I was married and had an infant son. While I was still working at the church, I started writing my own album. After that, as I changed and my life changed, I branched out spiritually and, as that happened, my tether to the church started to unravel. Also at that time were the rumblings of the end of my first marriage. There was a lot of deep change in my life those years.

Who I am now still has its roots in my Jesuit experience. It's been a very good and long road, and I've done things I said I would never do. Everything has left me feeling a sense of awe about life and very happy. At first, I thought I was going to be a Jesuit for the rest of my life and then that I was going to be married for the rest of my life. There is this amazing sense of looking at it in retrospect.

Do you still play music?

I don't do music very much. I noodle on my guitar once in a while. I developed a really wonderful and enjoyable sense of enjoyment for poetry and I have dabbled in writing poetry; it has become more of an outlet for me. I was never as driven by music the way John Foley was. Similarly, my son would probably curl up under a rock if he didn't have music.

I am an assistant store manager for REI, a company that sells outdoor gear. The outdoors has always been a central passion of my life. I'm a bit of a climber, kayaker and cyclist. I'm very lucky to be paid to do this. REI is a fantastic, Seattle-based company and does an excellent job of walking the talk relative to environmentalism. I have a situation of loving what I do for a living, and it is not at all what I'd have thought I'd be doing.

What are your images of God?

The spiritual tradition in my life that I'm closest to is Buddhism. In traditional theological terms, my strongest sense of God is the sense of total immanence. What I long to do in my life, as I grow older and calmer, is to allow myself continually to experience more and more. That's one of the reasons I love the outdoors; it's a little easier there for me.

I'm continually amazed at how difficult it is to live and feel simply. Spirituality, for me, has largely become a matter of expanding awareness. I remember reading Lost Christianity. The author, Jacob Needleman, was having a conversation with someone who told him the highest spiritual state was knowing, from moment to moment, what spiritual state you are in. That's tough. How do you live without going to sleep, without being distracted?

What has the St. Louis Jesuit adventure been like for you?

It was an adventure in fidelity among a group of men, long before men began to wonder how to build relationships with one another. The Society of Jesus has always been a venue for that kind of work among men. Our year-in, year-out effort to create something together, specifically as a group of composers, performers and educators added elements of continuity and intensity. When we did things just right, we did them together. When we blew it, that was part of the work relationship, too.

It was a unique adventure in creativity and self-expression. From the beginning, almost every note of our music was to be given away. Our focus was on liturgical music, music for use. We continually tempered the amount of self in that self-expression. There is something peculiar, something formative, not only to a song but to its composer — at least I tell myself so — when one of the final judgments on effectiveness is not how it sounds for the composer but for as many others as possible. In a sense then, the vast majority of our music, the St. Louis Jesuit music, was never ours anyway.

It was an adventure learning to accept this enormous gift. I'm not talking about our individual musicality, though I guess there was that. It's more a sense that, everywhere we went, as musicians, composers and liturgical educators, was ultimately a surprise and gift. Imagine being given the capacity, even if only for a short time, to speak with clarity and feeling both to and for a group of people, it doesn't matter how large or small, to know that you've been granted a moment (or for that matter, over ten years of moments) during which you've touched folks in all kinds of circumstances. You've touched them at the very heart of what they sense as being most important to them and their families. We were somehow able to help them give voice to that heart in celebration and in sorrow. That is what we were given. At our very best, we just got out of the way and we passed it along.

Roc O'Connor, S.J.

*T*here were two guys a year ahead of me who showed me a lot about guitar. They were very patient and, once I got into it, I really liked playing. I played for liturgies, and we had a novice rock-and-roll band. It was called Mogen David and the Grapes of Wrath. It was great fun.

"What a beautiful legacy you've given God's people!"

Theresa Donohoo
Vocalist and Recording Artist

My initial involvement in music ministry began as a result of a recruitment talk given by our handsome new deacon at Mass one Sunday morning. He was forming a folk group and needed singers. At fifteen, I suddenly heard the call to share my gifts with the community! Because I grew up in St. Louis, our repertory relied heavily on the new music of the St. Louis Jesuits. I recall my amazement when I began to notice that the lyrics were taken directly from Scripture. I mean, this was the 70s and being a good Catholic schoolgirl, what did I know from the Bible? It has been my privilege to share this wonderful, prayerful music with many congregations on many different occasions through the years. What a beautiful legacy you've given God's people! —T.D.

How did you get interested in music? What were your early experiences and influences?

It's funny, in a way. My family was not very musical at all. We had four records in the house when I was growing up. One was music from South Pacific, *one was Beethoven's 5th Symphony and one was the Nutcracker Suite. I remember putting them on the record player, turning them up loud and imagining I was conducting the orchestra.*

What I wanted to do was be a drummer and play rock-and-roll. As a family with a ton of kids and a small house, my parents thought, rather wisely, they weren't going to get me drums. They got me an electric guitar, and I started to learn in high school. I mainly learned when I entered the novitiate. There were two guys a year

ahead of me who showed me a lot about guitar. They were very patient and, once I got into it, I really liked playing it. I played for liturgies, and we had a novice rock-and-roll band. It was called Mogen David and the Grapes of Wrath. It was great fun. Schutte was a year ahead of me. I was learning to play as he was learning to compose.

Pete Townsend was my biggest influence. I just loved the way he played. He had a very primal sense of rhythm, power and grit. Gutsy-type stuff, especially in the rock opera Tommy. *Such great chord movement and writing. I also liked, very broadly, the rock-and-roll tradition and folk music. Dylan, Peter, Paul and Mary, stuff like that. Back then, people would sit around and sing throughout an evening. That was a way of being together.*

Help me understand what happened after *Lord of Light*. You're all together, and then a few years later you put out a last album. What were some of the pieces of that?

We moved up to Seattle in the summer of 1980. I, at thirty, began a bachelor's music program there. Bob and Dan took other courses, and John was working on an oratorio. We weren't writing a lot of liturgical music at the time. We were working so hard on learning to relate together, and that took energy away from composition.

Developing our relationships in the group was part of our reason for going to Seattle. (The other was to study music.) We were trying, especially in the second year there, to work on relating and relatedness. We decided that, in order to work as a group, we were going to have to work on communicating better. We spent many hours talking about who we were and trying to relate to each other. Even when Dan moved to Marquette University in 1982, while the rest of us stayed in Seattle, we wrote letters every month or so, summaries of what was going on, just to keep that communication going.

In the summer of 1983, John went to tertianship in Spokane, Duff came to Creighton, I went to Mankato and Tim stayed in Seattle. We kept writing letters and, in January 1984, we came back for a meeting to see what the next step was. Tim said he didn't want to be part of the group anymore, that he didn't want to continue with music. We were blown away. It was hard.

In 1985, Dan and I began tertianship. At the beginning of the summer of 1986, about the week before tertianship, Dan and I had lunch. He told me he'd been struggling a lot. He said that he'd decided to leave the Society. This was quite a surprise. The experience of that was hard, especially after having had these times of getting together and making commitments to each other. These hard times strained our relationships. Though we'd grown together, there was also a part of each person wanting to be more expressive in his own right about music and, in one sense, have a little less oversight. One of the good aspects of our separation was that people went on to discover their own style and voice, to explore what it means to compose in the church's life in the mid-1980s and early 1990s. The goal was to grow in the knowledge and the craft of composition, and each of us went in different paths along those lines.

What sort of a path have you taken since?

Part of the shift for me happened in the mid-1990s. When I was at Weston, I did my thesis on sacred space and the Bible. The most influential thing was a seminar with Jesuit Father Peter Fink on the philosophy of John Macmurray. The issues that really arose for me was how liturgy is truly an encounter of persons. It hadn't been that for me in a way that was satisfying. As a liturgical musician, my growing sense of boredom with it all prompted me to say, "I have to figure out what this stuff means or leave it. There has to be more depth in this than I'm realizing."

Coming to understand some of the tradition helped me refine my vision of liturgy. Reading courses about liturgical catechesis from a pastoral point of view and bringing in my own experience also helped. All of this prompted my way of teaching and the courses I teach, which have a fair amount of experiential data to them.

I think it's very important to continue pointing to ways that will, hopefully, set some conditions for the possibility that people can deepen their prayer at liturgy and increase their presence to God, themselves and others. The biggest thing we need to do is a kind of a catechesis, a very broad-looking catechesis that still draws its theological foundation from the Second Vatican Council. We could write some music but, more and more, the key element is still going to be catechesis. It seems that middle America, middle and upper class Catholics, middle and upper class Christians, have a danger of becoming irrelevant because we're not addressing the deepest part of people's experience. That is a part of coming to the edge, of talking to people in their joys and in their sorrows, in their heights and in their depths. That's what we all want to be about; that's certainly what I want to be about. It is an invitation to people to deepen the experience of their relationship to God, themselves and others.

Preparing the ground is that act of hope. I teach 20-year-olds and don't know what they're going to be like, what the church is going to be like, in twenty or thirty years, but maybe some of this will have a good effect on them.

What are some recurrent themes or images or feelings you find you often draw on?

There's a phrase that comes up a lot about the name of God — "Blessed be the name of God" — but I don't know what it means. I hope it's not just a filler. As far as themes are concerned, a lot of the music I wrote early on tended to be exhortative: "Seek the Lord," "Trust in the Lord," "Bless the Lord." What I've done more consciously in the last five years is strive to write more pieces that are second person.

I have this sense, from playing my own music or other people's, of trying to find the edge. Both a quiet song, like Foley's "Holy God" or my "Jesus the Lord," or an upbeat song, like "Lift Up Your Hearts," reflect that songs do what they need to do. Songs such as "Holy God" the way Foley has arranged it allow the feelings of reverence, longing and resistance to be there. Part of it, for me, both in performance and composition, is about trying to find the truth of a piece; it's at that

place where everything comes together. All of those positive and negative feelings come together. In Dufford's song "Save Us, O Lord," to really experience the ache and the frustration in the performance is what I find to be part of the truth of that piece. It has an edge; there's a sharpness to it.

How do you feel about getting back together? What are you hoping to accomplish?

We see it as an act of hope to work together, an act of reconciliation. It's also saying we've come to the sense that we can be more effective as a group than as individuals. The sum is greater than its parts, and there's something apostolically more vital, more compelling, about working as a group rather than as individuals. It's for the sake of advancing the music.

I think what we've always wanted to do and what we've tried to work for is the integration of horizontal and vertical, of the immanent and the transcendent. In coming together, we're making a restatement of that, saying this is important for the maturation of the church in the United States. It's about integrating what can be perceived as opposites. A good thing about the current work of the Vatican is its call back to a sense of reverence and transcendence. While some can fall into mere rubricism, the Vatican II renewal calls us to a deeper sense of community in the body of Christ, active in the world.

What has the St. Louis Jesuit adventure been like for you?

When I entered the Jesuits in 1967, I did not start out to be a composer of liturgical music. I had been strongly influenced by the Jesuits who taught me at Creighton Preparatory in Omaha, and so I thought I would teach high school until I actually did. I did not start out to serve the church as a musician, liturgist or composer of liturgical music. I eventually came to receive, acknowledge and accept the blessing and burden of this vocation within a vocation after many years as a Jesuit. My story does not begin with me living out a plan or dream that I had to compose music. Rather, my story is about me trusting in providence by walking through doors of opportunity that opened at the right time. I remember recognizing that pattern for the first time and learning to have confidence in it during my studies in St. Louis in the early 1970s.

As I look back on it now, I see that, in my teens and early twenties, I was more concerned with performing music with and for others at Mass. I was concerned about the group experience, that is, I got something out of Mass by doing, by being part of a group that could affect the whole congregation. As a young man, it seemed that the Mass was meant mainly to inspire the worshiping community by means of the word, especially the preaching, and to nourish us through the experience of Communion. Much of the early music of the liturgical reform fostered the worshiping community's awareness of itself as a living body, characterized by a drive to make the world a better place and by an intuitive feeling together. This orientation fit with and shaped my own experience of liturgy. A good Mass meant that everyone left with a sense of having participated in a meaningful act.

I ended up spending six weeks in Berkeley during the summer of 1974 with Dufford, Foley, Manion, Schutte and several Missouri Province novices studying music. Even after recording Neither Silver Nor Gold *the year before, I had no real plans to compose liturgical music. I am still not sure why or how I ended up traveling out there with them for the summer gathering.*

The morning after John Foley wrote "Come to the Water" and shared it in our evening music session, I opened the Scriptures to that passage, Isaiah 55, and found the words, "Seek the Lord while he may be found." Fifteen minutes later, and much to my amazement, "Seek the Lord" was born. I needed help to notate it since my own musical knowledge was quite lacking. The others encouraged me to try again. The next week I wrote "Trust in the Lord." I still didn't take myself seriously as a composer. Two songs do not a composer make! It would take many more years and studies for me to accept this calling to be a composer.

Dan Schutte

In grade school and high school, I was one of the geeks who played in the band; I played clarinet and saxophone. I didn't pick up the guitar until I was a junior in high school. It was the days of Simon and Garfunkel and I got hooked on their music.

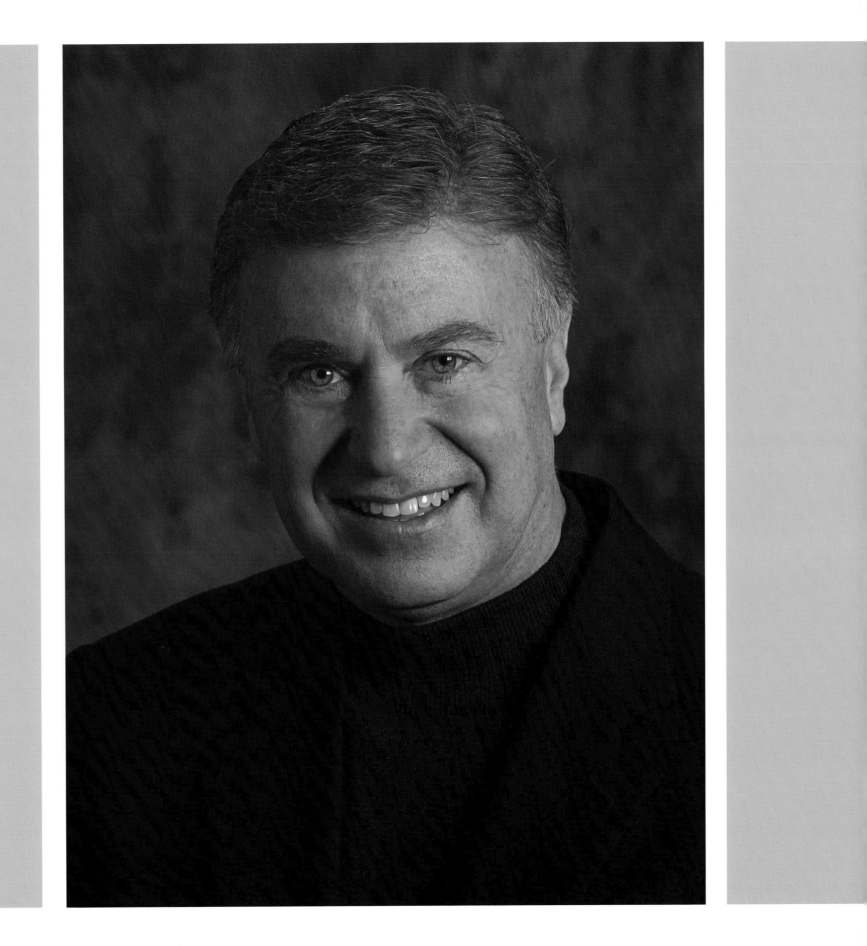

"I have never doubted that their music's blessed by the Holy Spirit"

Andy Alexander, S.J.
Vice-president for University Ministry
Director of Collaborative Ministry
Creighton University

128

I entered the Society of Jesus with Dan Schutte. We were in St. Louis during the amazing years — after Vatican II, during the Vietnam War — studying philosophy while learning the power of liturgy.

My personal relationship with my brothers transcends their music. They are simply great people, great friends and great ministers. Their music came from their individual prayer and encounter with passages of Scripture that spoke to their hearts. Particular songs seemed to be written to express that faith experience. At other times, pieces were written when their experiences of liturgy demanded something new, something deeper or something that people could sing and pray. I have never doubted that their music has been blessed by the Holy Spirit, so great has been the impact of their prayerful creativity upon the celebration of liturgy. — **A.A., S.J.**

What did you want to be growing up?

I wanted to be a pediatrician. That was my plan into high school, until I met some Jesuits and they influenced me in another direction. When I was at Marquette High, the priesthood was in the back of my mind, but I didn't give it a lot of thought until senior year. Up until that point I was set to go to medical school at Marquette University. That was the plan.

How did you get involved with liturgical music?

In grade school and high school, I was one of the geeks in the band; I played clarinet and saxophone. I didn't pick up the guitar until I was a junior in high school. It was the days of Simon and Garfunkel, and I got hooked on their music. One of my great influences was Jesuit Father John Eagan, who taught at Marquette High for many years. He loved to take groups of guys out camping along the shores of Lake Superior. At night we'd build a fire after dinner, I'd pull out a guitar and we'd sing folk songs for hours. This was an outlet for my interest in music; it motivated me to learn more.

I entered the Jesuit novitiate after high school with that music background. In the novitiate, there were some very fine guitarists in my class and I'd learn from them. It was at the time guitars were being introduced into the Mass; we were permitted to do that. I, along with others, began to introduce guitar-accompanied music into the liturgy.

The biggest influence on my music at this time was a classmate of mine from Omaha, Bill Laird. He and I had about the same level of musical ability, and we had the same inner sense and love for music. During our free time, which wasn't much, we'd sneak down to the trunk room, the room in the basement where they stored all the luggage. Nobody could hear us down there. We'd play the guitar, learn new songs and, eventually, began to write little pieces and bring them to each other for critique and encouragement.

I'd never written music before in my life, except to make up little melodies as I'd sit at my grandfather's piano. We had this gentle Jesuit, Father Barney Portz, on the faculty. He was a big influence on Roc, Duff and me. He taught mathematics but was also a musician. He was the choir director, and he recognized musical gifts in us. He'd corner us after we'd finished doing the breakfast dishes and take us down the trunk room where he'd give us singing lessons. He'd look at these pieces that Bill Laird and I had composed and he'd offer us his comments and suggestions. At some point he'd say, "You know, I think it's ready for us to try at Mass; let's see what happens." He was really the one who first saw the possibility of my music and encouraged me. He asked me to direct the choir and taught me how to do that.

Who were your early influences?

Simon and Garfunkel; Peter, Paul and Mary; Gordon Lightfoot; Rogers and Hammerstein; Lerner and Lowe. Later on it was the Beatles. The style of Peter, Paul and Mary especially fit the style of music we might be able to do at Mass. Many of their songs grew out of the folk tradition — that is, music that is meant to be sung by people, ordinary people. Most folk music was never written down but passed from family to family and generation to generation. It was music that people learned by heart and would sit around and sing together. That's exactly what we do at Mass, in a very simplified way. It was music for people to sing together and less for people to sit and listen to.

What was your first song?

One of the first songs that I wrote was a "Hail Mary" that has never been published. We sang it a few times at Mass. There were a few pieces from that very early time that have made it. One is "You are My Sons" that, for inclusive language reasons, later became "Before the Sun Burned Bright." When I was writing my Advent and Christmas album, I took the melody of that piece and changed the words to make it an Advent piece.

What did you do after the St. Louis Jesuits split up?

At about the same time that we decided to go our own ways, I made the decision to leave the Society of Jesus. In many ways, I loved being a Jesuit priest — my life is still steeped in the spirituality of St. Ignatius — but there was a really important part of my soul that was so unhappy and very alone. I'm sure that some people looking from the outside thought I was making a colossal mistake. Many were shocked and disappointed, and many didn't understand that this was simmering in me from my time in Berkeley eight years earlier.

Leaving the Jesuits was the most difficult decision I have ever made in my life; it wasn't that I was angry at the Society of Jesus or didn't love the priesthood. Rather, there was a great need for intimacy in my life that was so strong that I knew that I would be losing myself if I did not pay attention to it. I was terrified of leaving; I had no idea how I was going to do that, but I knew there was a part of my soul that needed it. I needed to get out of that structure.

I left at the end of the school year, and I lived with my folks for two months until I could find an apartment. I was so afraid and didn't sleep much for many weeks. I just had to ask God to figure this all out for me because I didn't know how it was going to work. One of the first things that happened was I got a call from the Wisconsin Province of the Society of Jesus. They said they wanted to return ownership to me of all my copyrights. As a Jesuit, the royalties for my music had gone directly to my Province. It was a very generous thing for them to do. At the time, it gave me a bit of security knowing there would be some income coming in. Then I got a call from a pastor who had heard I might be looking for work. He wondered if I would be willing to serve as music director for a few months. Those three or four months turned into a year, so God was certainly taking care of me.

During the next year, I began my first solo collection of music. Since then, I've done seven solo albums: Lover of Us All, Drawn by a Dream, Always and Everywhere, Glory In the Cross, You Are Near, Here I Am, Lord *and* Prince of Peace. *In 1999, I moved to San Francisco where I now make my home. I started working at the University of San Francisco five years ago. I am Composer in Residence, and I am a member of the University Ministry Office. I work as the director of liturgical music, mentoring student singers and musicians and preparing them for future ministry. I also travel, giving concerts and workshops. It is a privilege to meet many good people who love music and want to use their gifts in the service of their communities.*

What was the experience of the NPM convention like for you?

It was a very moving experience. Some people have used the word "magical" to describe it. While on the stage with Bob, John and Roc, I had a hard time singing. There were moments when I just got all choked up. I don't think any of us expected it. We were part of a program celebrating the twenty-fifth anniversary of the National Association of Pastoral Musicians in Washington, DC. In the months preceding the event, the planners asked if we'd be willing to do "City of God" as part of the program. They placed the song at the end of the event. When it came time, the narrators announced that they wanted to welcome four composers who hadn't sung together publicly for many years. As the four of us walked up on stage, everyone in the hall stood up. What I noticed was that, as we began the introduction to "City of God," everyone put down their printed programs. Nobody needed to look at their music for this song; it was part of their musical bones. It was so touching to look into people's faces. They sang, many with their eyes closed, from the bottom of their souls. It was a wonderful, grace-filled moment of celebrating with all these people. It was something beautiful God did in us and through us. You could see it in people's faces.

Afterward, as they reflected on the event, the folks at Oregon Catholic Press recognized that something special had happened that day. They were as surprised as we were at people's response. I believe it was, for all of us, one of those defining moments that we could not ignore. We were led, in the next months and years, to discern what it meant.

What are your images of God?

I have so many images. There is a wonderful story about a father, called to school because his daughter got sick and threw up all over her school uniform. He ran into the school. Before the Sister could say anything, he grabbed up his little daughter and said "Honey, don't worry, it's going to be okay." Of course, by doing that, he soiled his business suit. What a wonderful image of God as someone who doesn't worry about getting our mess all over himself. He wants us to know that, in the end, everything is going to be okay.

In many ways, my images of God come from a wonderful mother. I knew that there was someone in this world who — regardless of what I did, what roads I took, no matter how I messed up or even what good I did — was never was going to turn away. It was the kind of grounded love you never have to question. There's the feminine image of God for me who is kind of like that mother. There's nothing that can separate us.

I love the image of God in the Hebrew Testament book Song of Songs: the God who is in love with us — so in love with us that God can hardly stand it — and just wants to be close. In my song "You Are Near" from Psalm 139, I talk about two images of God that are important to me. One is the God who knows us through and through. Even when we can't figure ourselves out, God knows us. We don't have to speak the words and yet God knows what's in our hearts. The other image that I love from that psalm is the God who doesn't wait in the "wings of our lives" until we're ready to come and pay a visit. Ours is a God who pursues us, who comes after us, and is so in love with us that waiting is not an option.

What has the St. Louis Jesuit adventure been like for you?

There are times when we just don't have a clue about our path in life. As a young Jesuit, I majored in psychology and my peers told me I was crazy. "Dan, you should be pursuing music," they would say. I told them music for me was a hobby, was just for fun, but that it was not the center of my life. Little did I know that music would indeed become my life's work and passion. It just goes to show how many people have clearer insight into our future and purpose than we can see ourselves.

I could never have imagined I would someday be sitting here writing my reflections on thirty years of collaboration with this unlikely group of composers. I also never imagined that any music I would write could find such a place of honor in people's lives and become part of the church's treasure of sacred music. Back then, I knew only that I loved music and that it was an expression of my soul.

When in the Jesuit novitiate, I began writing pieces for the liturgy, but I never would have continued these stumbling attempts at music had it not been for the encouragement of my Jesuit peers and superiors. Those early pieces have, luckily, never seen the light of day but, somewhere in the midst of my stumbling, there were people who recognized something of beauty and value. As I continued to write, little by little, I learned more about the craft of composition.

At the start of our adventure, I was shy, hesitant and unsure of myself. I did have, however, some inkling that I had a gift for creating music that people liked to sing. The group collaboration grounded me as I grew my wings. Even before I met him, John Foley's music was an inspiration to me. Some of John's early pieces had been brought to our community by visiting Jesuits. I was so excited to see another person writing music for the liturgy in a contemporary style. It was good and, like my own, based on Scripture. Best of all, it was music I found could help me pray and worship.

Over the years, I've learned so much from Bob, John, Roc and Tim. Each one has made his special contribution to the music of the group. Each has written music I admire and have held up as something to strive for in my own writing. Even more than that, they've all taught me about God. The journey of our companionship has been one of grace and growth. Growth is most often accompanied with pain, and the path was not always easy. We are each flawed, sinful human beings trying to find our way. Sometimes we hurt each other deeply. There were always misunderstandings that needed to be resolved. The amazing thing is we persevered together and continued to work with each other for nearly fifteen years before we separated. There are not many music groups that stay together that long. What is more remarkable is that, after twenty years, we made the decision two years ago to come together once more for this reunion recording.

Lord, teach me to be generous.

Teach me to serve you as you deserve;

To give and not to count the cost;

To fight and not to heed the wounds;

To toil and not to seek for rest;

To labor and not to ask for reward;

Save that of knowing that I do your will.

St. Ignatius of Loyola

Roc O'Connor, S.J., Dan Schutte, Rev. Bill Byron, S.J., President of University of Scranton, Bob Dufford, S.J., and Tim Manion

In 1980, The University of Scranton, Pennsylvania, in recognition of their extraordinary contribution to the worship of the contemporary church, awarded the St. Louis Jesuits an honorary doctoral degree. The photo above shows the Jesuits with Fr. William Byron, S.J., the president of the university. John Foley was studying music in England at the time and unable to attend the ceremony.

THE SAINT LOUIS JESUITS

Prayer is the center of every Jesuit's life. Prayer is what the Jesuit strives to cultivate in the lives of others. Ignatius of Loyola wanted his Jesuit sons to find God in all things, to be contemplatives in action. Their prayer flows over into works. Their works reach out in service to their fellow human beings in all parts of the world.

It is a privileged work that creates an atmosphere for prayer. It is all the more privileged and special when the work produces words and music capable of carrying sacred scripture into the hearts of young believers.

Midway in the decade of the 1970s, the centuries-old Jesuit tradition of prayer and service was enriched and advanced by five young men whose talent matched their vision of providing for the contemporary Church a fresh environment for liturgical prayer. Singers and composers, brought together for seminary study on the campus of Saint Louis University, the now famous Saint Louis Jesuits wrote and sang their songs to help others draw closer to God. In particular, these creative artists hoped to create for their campus contemporaries an opportunity to sing ancient prayers in a modern idiom. Their success surpassed their fondest hopes.

This University Community knows The Saint Louis Jesuits by their works and welcomes them on this day made all the more memorable by their presence and their songs.

It is with great admiration and appreciation of their service to the Church that the President and Trustees of this Jesuit University, in solemn convocation assembled and in accord with our chartered authority. legally proclaim

ROBERT DUFFORD
JOHN FOLEY
TIMOTHY MANION
ROBERT O'CONNOR
DANIEL SCHUTTE

Doctors of Humane Letters, Honoris Causa

That they may enjoy all the rights and privileges of this our highest honor, we have issued these letters patent under our hand and the corporate seal of the University on this twenty-fifth day of May, in the ninety-second year of the University and in the Year of Our Lord One Thousand Nine Hundred and Eighty.

Marilyn Coar
Secretary

William J Byron, S.J
President

Some people grew up watching American Bandstand, Elvis, Peter, Paul and Mary, the Beatles and even Monty Python. I, like so many of my generation, grew up liturgically on the music of the St. Louis Jesuits. I remember feeling that, at last, we had a repertoire of liturgical music that was scripturally-based, singable by the assembly and accessible to burgeoning pastoral guitarists. The Jesuits' music was and is truly a gift from God.

I still own my split-edged and dog-eared albums of *Neither Silver Nor Gold*, *Earthen Vessels*, *A Dwelling Place*, *Gentle Night* and others. I have memories of my parish community being carried through pain with "Be Not Afraid" and of claiming our gifts through "Here I Am, Lord." We offered ourselves to God through "I Lift Up My Soul" and united with the poor and the disenfranchised through "The Cry of the Poor." We praised down the rafters with "Lift Up Your Hearts!" The scriptural texts touched our hearts as never before through the music of Bob, Dan, John, Roc and Tim. But this music did more. It accompanied our community as we faced racial integration on the southwest side of Chicago, as we weathered the scorn of local pastors who viewed our parish community as draining their Sunday collections and as we eventually faced parish closure in order to be leaven for other communities.

Thank you, guys, for holding us up and caring for us as heralds of God's love and mercy!

Dr. Dolly Sokol
Director of the Office of Worship
Archdiocese of Santa Fe

"Sing a New Song Unto the Lord" is not only the name of one of the better known songs of the St. Louis Jesuits, it is also an apt describer of what they did for English-speaking Christians all over the world. If not a an entirely new song, the St. Louis Jesuits gave us a new and inspiring musical idiom deeply rooted in the biblical texts, rich in metaphor, prayerful in tone and artfully arranged for congregational singing. They have done more than any single group or individual to assist pastors in fulfilling the duty imposed by Vatican II, "to ensure that the faithful take part knowingly, actively and fruitfully"[Sacred Liturgy, #11] in all liturgical celebrations. Their music invites us to experience the holy.

Stephen Privett, S.J.
President, University of San Francisco

St. Louis Jesuits receiving Distinguished Alumni Award at St. Louis University, 1983

A Time For Reunion

$\mathcal{A}$t its national convention during the summer of 2001, the National Association of Pastoral Musicians celebrated its 25th anniversary. At the same time, it celebrated the retirement of its founder, Rev. Virgil Funk. One of the many events on the program for the week was a retrospective of the music of the past twenty-five years. A small group of musicians accompanied the audience through selections chosen to represent the most significant music of this time. The music was interspersed with a historical commentary. Near the end of the program the commentators announced, "We'd now like to call on stage a group of men who've contributed enormously to the prayerful worship of Christian churches throughout the world.

St. Louis Jesuits at the National Association of Pastoral Musicians' Convention, July 2001

They haven't sung together on stage for nearly twenty years. Ladies and gentlemen, please welcome The St. Louis Jesuits." The response was immediate and unmistakable. People rose to their feet as Bob Dufford, John Foley, Roc O'Connor and Dan Schutte stepped onto the stage. The joyful, driving musical introduction to "City of God" began. For the next four minutes, hundreds of voices raised the roof of the Omni-Shoreham ballroom with song. Many, including the Jesuits, sang with tears in their eyes. No one needed to look at the printed program; the words and melody were part of everyone's musical memory. When the song ended, the applause continued for a very long time.

The Jesuits were as surprised as anyone by the response to their appearance at the convention. They were overwhelmed to know people still had such a response to their music. Roc O'Connor wondered if God's message for them was to consider a new recording project. It took them several years to finally sit down and talk. In October 2003, they gathered in San Francisco to discern what to do. They spent a week discussing the possibility of another recording and doing what they loved most, sharing new music with each other. They decided to join forces, one more time, to offer new songs of hope and encouragement.

St. Louis Jesuits with John Limb, Publisher of Oregon Catholic Press, November 2004

Greetings all,

Here's a thought that's been rumbling around in my mind since last summer. Singing together on stage for the first time in twenty years was a special blessing. It was nice to receive the adulation, but what really was consoling was playing and singing with you guys. Several folks came up after that event and talked to me about us getting together for a concert.

I'm not sure about that, but for the first time since OCP brought us back out to Portland to record some older *Neither Silver Nor Gold* songs, I feel like there's a need to talk about doing something together. I don't know what that something is. What do we have to offer now that we didn't then? Do any of you have any desire to darken each others' door anymore? There are options that we can talk about. Any takers?

I'm guessing that we'll all be there in St. Louis for the Composers' Forum. Do you want to go for a walk, a beer, some warm milk or some Ovaltine? If we all can't make it to St. Louis this time, do you want to have a phone conversation about it sometime soon? These are some reflections and options. Thanks for even thinking about this, guys. God bless you in your living, praying, ministering and, well, living. See ya soon!

— **Email message sent by Roc O'Connor to the other St. Louis Jesuits, January 2002**

*Portland, Oregon
in November 2004*

Nothing is more practical
than finding God;
that is, than falling in love
in a quite absolute, final way.
What you are in love with,
what seizes your imagination,
will affect everything.
It will decide what will get you
out of bed in the morning,
what you will do with your evenings,
how you will spend your weekends,
what you read, who you know,
what breaks your heart,
and what amazes you with joy and gratitude.
Fall in love; stay in love,
and it will decide everything.

Pedro Arrupe, S.J.
Superior General of the Society of Jesus, 1961-1984

St. Louis Jesuits, Portland 2004

*M*y first introduction to liturgical music was in 1975. During my senior year of high school, I participated in a search retreat and, since I played guitar, was volunteered along with a classmate to lead music at the retreat liturgies. I had only been playing guitar for a couple years; along with my limited ability to play the instrument came an even more limited repertoire of songs. I quickly pulled out my binder of tunes and looked for anything that might pass for church music. Out came an assortment of titles by the Beatles, Cat Stevens, and Simon and Garfunkel that somehow managed to pass muster with my fellow retreatants and our priest leader.

Given the apparent success of my first foray into music ministry, I was invited back for the monthly follow-up Masses. This invitation was accompanied by a very fortuitous happening. A friend passed along to me a slim volume of Catholic folk music titled *Songs of Praise and Reconciliation* and published by North American Liturgy Resources (NALR) of Cincinnati. (This book was the precursor to NALR's eventual best-selling hymnal *Glory & Praise*.)

This book was a godsend to me. Among the fifty or so titles were a handful of songs by a group of composers who were referred to in the back of the book as the St. Louis Jesuits. Such well-known titles as "Let Heaven Rejoice," "For You Are My God" and "Sing a New Song" found their way into my hands and into the pews of many Catholic parishes thanks to this wonderful little book. Equipped as I was, with this music and my guitar, there was no looking back. The rest, as they say, is history.

I can't begin to capture what the music of the St. Louis Jesuits has meant to me. This music filled not just a void in Catholic liturgical music, but a void in my own life during those very formative teen and young adult years.

I wasn't just learning songs (and, thanks to the performance notes, how to play better guitar); I was learning Scripture. To this day, I can't think of Psalm 139 without also thinking of "You Are Near," read Galatians 3:38 without hearing "One Bread, One Body" or hear the injunction to "Be not afraid" without immediately recalling Bob Dufford's timeless setting of these words.

Equally profound for me was the effect that this music had on others. I saw early on how other people were also opened to Scripture or helped through various life challenges by the power of this music. I learned that, through music, lives can be changed in profound ways. It was this realization that led to my eventual decision to choose music ministry as my vocation and career.

My life has taken many turns these past thirty years. If people had told me in 1975 that someday I'd be the publisher of Oregon Catholic Press, I'd have said they were crazy. Yet here I am. I owe much to the St. Louis Jesuits, and I think it's safe to say that without the gift of their music, I'd not be where I am today. Thanks, guys!

John J. Limb
Publisher, Oregon Catholic Press
August 1, 2005

Summer 2005

After many months of planning, the group gathered at Dead Aunt Thelma's Recording Studio in Portland, Oregon, in July 2005 to begin recording their new collection. One of the most difficult decisions they had to make was choosing twelve pieces from over thirty new pieces. In the end, Bob, Dan, John and Roc each contributed three pieces to fill out the new collection, *Morning Light*.

One happy event of their reunion was having Tim Manion, who left the group in 1983, join them in Portland for four days. The others in the group had not seen Tim, who now lives in Phoenix, for over twenty years. What made their meeting even more special was having Tim join them in the studio to contribute his voice and guitar to the new recording. It was a wondrous and humbling moment as the five stood at microphones to sing together after so many years. The once familiar sound of their voices filled the room as they laid down the tracks for the new songs.

Portland, Oregon

Photos taken during recording of Morning Light, *Portland, Oregon, July 2005*

Bob Dufford

The iPod, iTunes and Finale were not even the stuff of a Buck Rogers dream when four young men set forth to create a musical medium for worship that was engaging and spiritually enlivening. They, like many of us, were stirred by the vision of communal worship set forth in the discussions and documents of Vatican II. Not unlike Lewis and Clark, it was to be a journey into an unknown new world. A former jewelry salesman in Cincinnati, Ohio, and a former seminarian set forth on the same journey bearing a banner that read "NALR." In the dark quarters of a former drugstore, the two energies meshed. Months later, on a warm Cincinnati summer evening, a summer song program concluded with the joyous Scripture strains of the St. Louis Jesuits.

We took the call for renewal, particularly of our prayer together, seriously. We used the best available resources that this new vision called forth. The Jesuits brought their pastoral, scriptural and musical gifts together, refined through the spiritual insights of the Society of Jesus.

As I look back, it was a time of hard work, probing faith and creativity that some do not, and probably never will, understand. For others, the time, the energy, the faith and the music were a welcome gift.

Bill Hartgen, Jr., S.S.
Director: Cooperative Ministries

The music of the St. Louis Jesuits forms the bulk of the soundtrack of my personal story as a Catholic. It's the music I sang and prayed with as I moved out of high school, through university and into adulthood.

Their musical settings of Scripture and Mass texts have enlivened the liturgies of my home parish in Idaho, the communities I have worshipped with in Rome and the congregations I have written about celebrating Mass with Pope John Paul II in English-speaking countries around the world. I'm not sure if the pope noticed, but I did when thousands of Jamaicans used steel drums and a calypso beat to make "Though the Mountains May Fall" their own during a 1993 Mass in Kingston.

Accessible and beautiful, the music has an uncanny ability to connect individuals and lift their prayers up together, fostering the harmony that is the church at worship and carrying me along with it.

Cindy Wooden
Senior Rome Correspondent
Catholic News Service

Recognizing that there is no monolithic Black African American religious experience and aware of any insider's appetite for aggrandizement, let me venture, nevertheless, to posit that music is in our Black sanctified soul. James Cone notes: "In Africa and America, black music was not an artistic creation for its own sake; it was directly related to daily life, work and play. Song was an expression of the community's view of the world and its existence in it. Through music, Africans recorded their history, initiated the young into adulthood, and expressed their religious beliefs." (*The Spirituals and the Blues: An Interpretation* [New York: Seabury, 1972], p. 32)

Equally important is the book — Sacred Scripture. For the Black African American community, the Bible "was not for our ancestors a mere record of the wonderful works of God in a bygone age; it was a present record of what was soon to come." It was a message that was heard and "we learned to celebrate it in the midst of sorrow, to hope in the depths of despair and to fight for freedom in the face of all obstacles." (See Joseph L. Hosze, et al., *What We Have Seen and Heard: A Pastoral Letter on Evangelization from the Black Bishops of the United States* [Cincinnati, OH: St. Anthony Messenger Press, 1984], p. 4-5)

What has been affirmed about music and Scripture in days gone by is no less true today. It should come as a surprise to no one that the music of the St. Louis Jesuits found a resonance in our community. Given the scriptural basis of their lyrics, the pastoral accessibility of their music and Black folks' genius at improvisation, their music continues to resound. Even Schutte's "Here I Am, Lord" is included in the classic cross-denominational *African American Heritage Hymnal*.

May their music in our community continue to echo to the building up of the church and God's greater glory.

J–Glenn Murray, S.J.
Director, Office for Pastoral Liturgy, Diocese of Cleveland
July 31, 2005
Feast of Saint Ignatius of Loyola

Tim Manion

Dan Schutte

It was the fall of 1982. In the Diocese of New Ulm in southern Minnesota we were beginning a process of renewal for the whole diocesan church. We were launching whole-community catechesis that year and we were keenly interested in helping adults hear their own call to faith and justice, indeed, their call to animate the world with the spirit of Christ. But how? How could we teach them about Moses and Samuel, Isaiah and Jeremiah, Mary of Nazareth and the pattern of their own divine call?

Enter Dan Schutte and the St. Louis Jesuits. Within months, most of our leaders were humming the great biblical story from Isaiah 6: "Who will bear my light to them; whom shall I send…? Here I am, Lord. Is it I, Lord? I have heard you calling in the night…" They had been catechized in a most powerful way! And that song still lingers on their lips to this day.

Bill Huebsch
President and Publisher
Twenty-Third Publications

In April of 1980, I chaired the first New England regional convention for National Association of Pastoral Musicians. In so many ways, it was one of the defining moments of my life. It was the first time I met and worked with Roc O'Connor and Dan Schutte. I entered the convention knowing little of their music. I was slightly behind the times. I remember being impressed by what I heard at that convention, but the impact of their music on me and on countless others, then and now, was summarized by a letter from a musician attending that convention. He stated that he thought the event was good but it didn't seem to touch his life. He beautifully recalled the closing event when Dan and Roc led the assembly in "You Are Near." He had been moved to tears. The music of the St. Louis Jesuits touched him in a way that no other music had during our five days together. For me that's the key to understanding the contribution of the music of the St. Louis Jesuits. It touches people's hearts and gives voice to the gentle and powerful word of God that nourishes our souls and strengthens our spirits.

Fr. Ronald E. Brassard
Chairman of Development Committee
National Association of Pastoral Musicians
Pastor, Immaculate Conception Parish, Cranston, RI

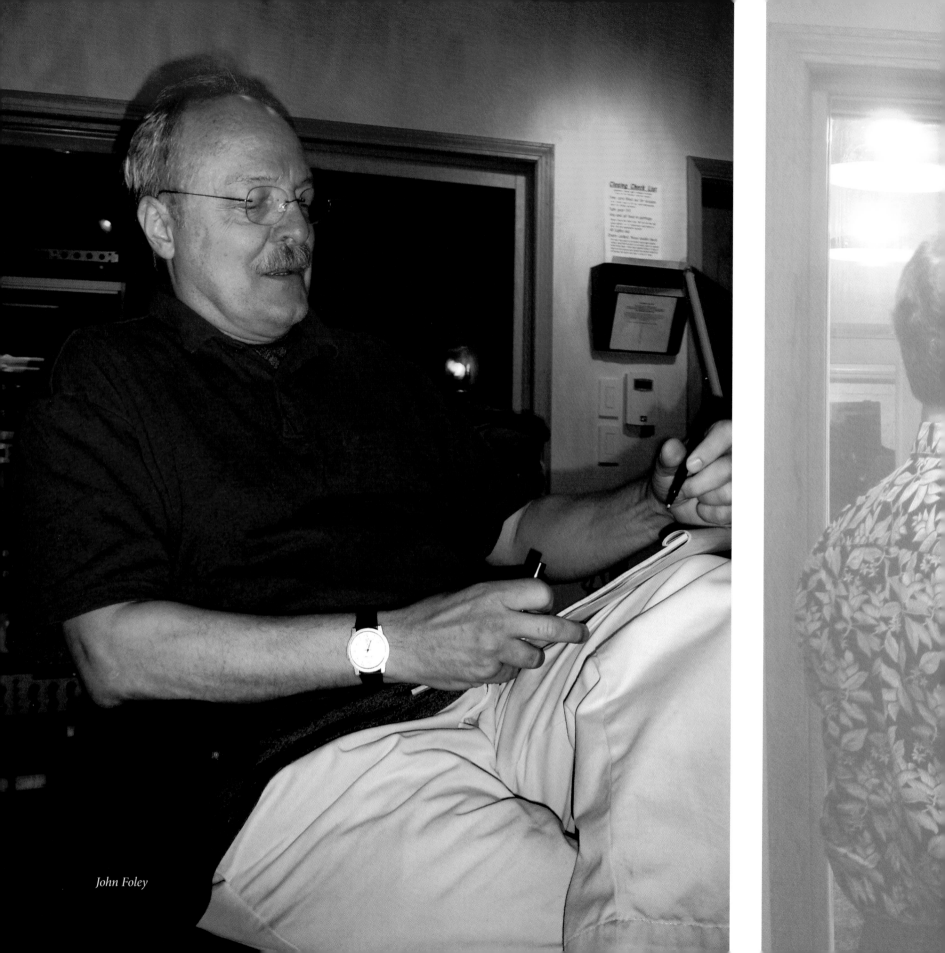

John Foley

Congratulations to our friends, the St. Louis Jesuits, on the occasion of their first new recording in twenty years and their thirtieth anniversary of composing music for the church.

"There Is a River" of song flowing through the church. It is a river that has reached to "All the Ends of the Earth." As "Earthen Vessels" who "Seek the Lord," this river of song has comforted us at times and urged us to "Be Not Afraid." It has invited us to "Come to the Water," "Lift Up Your Hearts" and give "Glory and Praise to Our God." We have been called to hear "The Cry of the Poor," to build the "City of God" and have stated emphatically our commitment to the Lord's service as we have sung "Here I Am, Lord." "You Are Near," "Holy Darkness" and "Take, Lord, Receive" have drawn us to deeper prayer and contemplation. The river has never run dry, and more recent offerings such as "Table of Plenty," "Meadows and Mountains" and "Behold the Glory of God" have continued to nourish us.

The impact of their songs on the church and our liturgies has been enormous. It has been a privilege to know them and to be their colleagues in creating music for the church.

Your companions on the journey,
Carol Jean Kinghorn-Landry and Carey Landry

Recently, the National Association of Pastoral Musicians conducted a national survey asking its members to name sixty liturgical songs that every American Catholic should know. It was no surprise that the list included a number of compositions by the St. Louis Jesuits.

The work of these composers, dating back to the 1970s, marked a milestone in the post-Vatican II development of music for the liturgy among English-speaking Catholics. These Jesuits took seriously the mandate of the Second Vatican Council for composers to focus their work on texts drawn from scriptural and liturgical sources.

Their numerous, well-crafted musical settings have met the test of time and really foster active participation. Their work marked a significant advance in music written for contemporary ensembles and demonstrated how liturgical assemblies could be led effectively and beautifully by choir and cantor with the accompaniment of acoustic and wind instruments. The inclusion of some of their best-known compositions in the hymnals of other Christian churches is a solid testimony to the importance of their contribution.

J. Michael McMahon
President, National Association of Pastoral Musicians

Roc O'Connor

How nice to honor these men who have done so much to help us pray the liturgy through the years! My personal acquaintance with the music of the St. Louis Jesuits came after most of the Catholic world already sang it quite extensively. I was busy using four-part harmony with my nuns' schola, and it was not until I went to St. Patrick's Seminary to work with the choir that I came to know and love this music. What a place this wonderful repertory has had in our development as Christians! Until these young men appeared, we were floundering, trying to find music that engaged, may I even say entertained, our young people. With them came music that was thoroughly grounded in good theology and Scripture. They helped us pray the Scriptures with lyricism and beauty. How deeply grateful we are to them!

Sr. Suzanne Toolan, RSM
Composer, Spiritual Director, Retreat Director

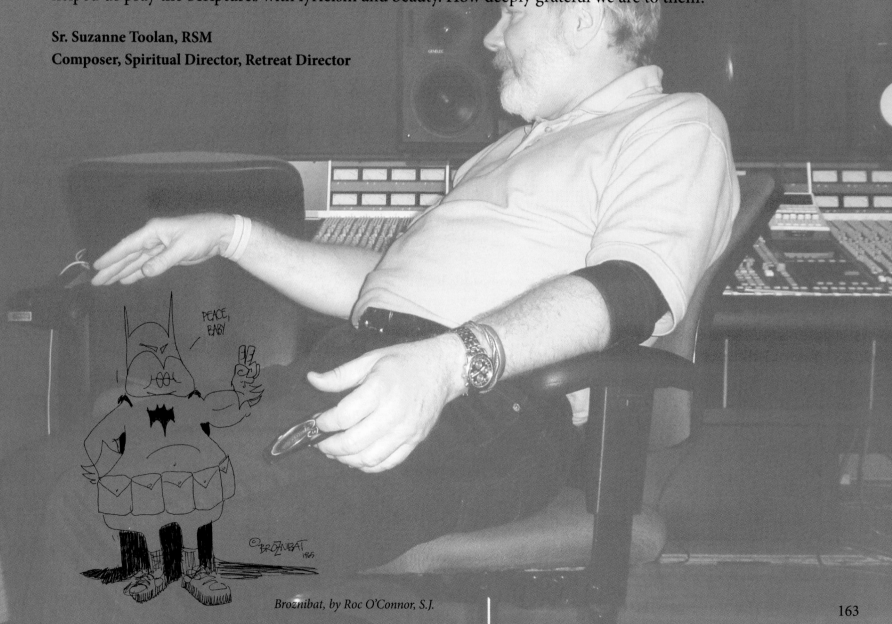

Broznibat, by Roc O'Connor, S.J.

Choir members during recording session   *Bob Dufford directing choir*

I was a latecomer to the St Louis Jesuits phenomenon. Though I'd been leading a choir since 1974, it was the late 1970s before a priest told me about your music, and when I said I wasn't aware of it, he looked at me like I was from another planet. Like the music of Gelineau, Proulx, Deiss, Repp, Peloquin, and Wise, it was formative for the American liturgical music experience. Solidly scriptural, rhythmic, hauntingly melodic, and utterly accessible, your music changed the way we experienced Sunday. Thank you for helping us find our voice.

Rory Cooney
Composer and Recording Artist

Producer, Kevin Walsh, directing string players

Roc O'Connor and John Foley

Music of the Soul

I wrote "Like a Shepherd" during the first summer we spent together as a group, in Berkeley. It was my one song for the summer. I had loved Handel's *Messiah* for many years and have often gone to the same Scripture passages in my own music, e.g., "Every Valley," "Worthy Is the Lamb," "Behold, I Tell You a Mystery" and "He Shall Feed His Flock Like a Shepherd." This last one refers to the passages in the book of Isaiah where the prophet speaks to those who think God's care for them is over: "Comfort, give comfort to my people" (Isaiah 40:1). "Go up on a high mountain, bring your glad tidings" (Isaiah 40:9). "He is like a shepherd feeding his flock, gathering the lambs in his arms, holding them against his breast, and leading them to their rest" (Isaiah 40:11).

Like the prophet, I wanted to paint God as one to whom people can entrust their lives. In "Like a Shepherd," the words and music present two contrasting images. In the refrain, we see a tender, calm image of a God who offers nourishment and comfort. Then the verses speed up and are more forceful. Both are images of God from the Old Testament. God is always a combination of strength and gentleness that cannot be separated.

"Worthy Is the Lamb" also offers this dual approach to our way of imagining God. In the refrain in 4/4 time, the sounds are big, like Roman legions marching in *Ben Hur*. They connote God's power, majesty and dominion. In contrast, the verses suddenly shift into 3/4 time and into a minor key. The aura is one of mystery and wonder. For me, this is a daily image of God who is both powerful and strong — yet mysterious and hidden — laboring for us very simply behind the scenes. Liturgy needs to bear the glory and grandeur, and also the intimacy and humbleness, of God. I believe this glory, grandeur and intimacy give us a sense of belonging. We are privileged to be part of something huge that stretches beyond our galaxy and to be known by someone who calls us by name and knows the number of hairs on our heads because they have been counted lovingly so often.

Bob Dufford, S.J.

"Like a shepherd he feeds his flock, and gathers the lambs in his arms, holding them carefully close to his heart, leading them home."

and gath-ers the lambs in His arms._____

"O, let all who thirst, let them come to the water.
And let all who have nothing, let them come to the Lord:
without money, without price. Why should you
pay the price, except for the Lord?"

O let all who thirst,

I wrote "Come to the Water" under what I thought were difficult circumstances. The rest of the group had just finished laughing at two pieces I had written. Okay, it was tender laughter — not the mocking kind — but it sent me up to my room somewhat grumpy. I knew they were right, but why? It hit me that I had written the two songs in a hurry, just to get something written. From this experience I got a perhaps obvious, but very important, insight. I must write music focused on what I care about, not just about anything.

I opened the *New American Bible* to the book of Isaiah, chapter 55, which I love. There were the words, "All you who are thirsty, come to the water! You who have no money, come, receive grain and eat; come without paying and without cost, drink wine and milk!" Because I could speak these words with conviction, I was able to work them into a hymn tune with a kind of revival flavor. My colleagues loved it, and so did I. I thought it was too melodically difficult for a congregation and more appropriate for choirs. Wow, was I wrong! The people in the pews took hold of it and never let go.

Why did the passage mean so much to me? I guess it was the freedom of the invitation contained in it: you don't have to stand back from God and starve, following all the rules but never being fed. God is all around you, brimming with love. Open your eyes and mouth and receive.

John Foley, S.J.

"Jesus....Jesus....Let all creation bend the knee to the Lord."

172

Beginning in the late spring of 1977, I found myself in my first deep, existential crisis. I lost at love and hurt like hell. I had just completed my first year of theology at the Jesuit School of Theology, Berkeley, CA. That summer we, the SLJ's, met in Phoenix to record songs for Advent and Christmas, a collection called *Gentle Night*. I remember feeling like my innards had been gouged out. I walked a lot in the early morning because I couldn't sleep. This experience stood in stark contrast to the goodness and grace of the recording session. I returned to Berkeley for the fall quarter and life continued marked by very good people, excellent classes, encouraging events, but always pulled by the undertow of grief and loss.

As I recall, it was that next autumn when I was back at Berkeley that I received this meditative piece that came to be titled "Jesus the Lord." I was still in grief. I still didn't sleep much. Yet I continued my studies and my involvement in the JSTB community of students and faculty. I maintained a fairly busy schedule as a mode of dealing with it all.

I had read about the "Jesus prayer" in *Journey of a Pilgrim* some time earlier, and it really touched me. I wondered whether or not it might be possible to find a vehicle for chanting the Holy Name at liturgy. But, this was a question that mainly stayed way back in my awareness. One night before trying to go to sleep, the song just appeared. It was there, whole cloth — the refrain, the accompaniment, and the overall ideas for all three verses! No planning it, no sitting down to compose, no collecting or sorting through texts to find the right sources.

I mainly remember being so tired that night that I told myself I need to remember this piece, and fell solidly asleep. Not only that, but I was so busy over the next few days that I couldn't take the time to put it all on paper. The real miracle is that I did not forget the lyrics, melody and chords. Two days later, I found the time to write it out. I played it right then just as I had heard it the first time. This is the only song that has ever been "given" to me. As a rule, I have to work at bringing a piece along from, say, a musical phrase, to a complete song. Like giving birth to a child, some labor pains are great and long, some are easy and quick. "Jesus the Lord" was the incredibly quick birth kind. And, I'm grateful for the gift.

Roc O'Connor, S.J.

Let all cre - a - tion bend the knee

In the late 1970s, I was studying theology in Berkeley, California. A fellow Jesuit came knocking on my door one day to ask a favor. "Dan, would you be willing to write a piece for the upcoming diaconate ordinations?" I'm sure he saw the anxious look on my face as it registered in my brain. This was Wednesday and the ordinations were on Saturday. I told him of my doubts, but I told him I would try. I prayed, "Lord, I really don't feel up to this. Please give me energy and the words and notes to put on this paper."

I worked for two days on "Here I Am, Lord." On Friday, we printed what I had done so the choir could rehearse that evening. I remember feeling doubtful about my efforts and was surprised and delighted that people found it to be so moving and prayerful. I had experienced the Divine Spirit, who overshadowed me and gave my simple efforts a power far beyond what I might be able to create.

The story doesn't end there. When I showed the piece to my music companions, Bob, John and Roc suggested there was something not quite right about the words to the refrain. I was stunned and initially resistant to make any changes. The original words I wrote were "Here I am, Lord. Here I stand, Lord. I have heard you calling in the night. I will go, Lord, where you lead me. I will hold your people in my heart." Bob, Roc and John all had the same reaction. "It just sounds a little too self-assured and confident, Dan." As I tried to listen to them, I realized they were right. That's not the way the biblical stories of the call of Samuel or Isaiah go. If anything, both of them were hesitant, doubtful of their ability to answer the call. "But, Lord, I don't know the words to speak" (Isaiah 50). I realized how true that is for all of us as we try to embrace God's call. The true story is that God is the one who makes up for all that we lack in ourselves. As St. Paul says, "We are strong in our weakness" (1 Corinthians 1:25). I decided to change the original lyrics I had written.

Dan Schutte

174

"Here I am, Lord. Is it I, Lord?
I have heard you calling in the night.
I will go, Lord, if you lead me.
I will hold your people in my heart."

I have heard my peo-ple cry.

Voices of Hope

All of us, young and old, need to know that there is hope. As we travel life's sometimes rocky journey, we reach for any signs of light and hope. Sometimes we reach for things that only give us a false hope, a temporary relief, from the hurt and the shadows that darken our souls. Perhaps one of the simple, humble things we can do is offer little glimpses of light and hope to each other. These small glimmers may be just what we need. We need each other to continue to dream dreams and see visions.

In recent years, things have shifted for me. Through my work at the Jesuit Retreat House in Oshkosh, I have found more hope for the church than ever before in my life. I don't find it in power moves within the hierarchical structure of the church or in large cultural movements, such as the Internet or mass media events; instead, I see it in people who come to the retreat house and call it home. I meet those who begin to take their spiritual lives seriously, not because they are commanded under pain of mortal sin or shunned by others, but because they want to. People share their stories about God. They deal with the challenges of their lives by turning to face their failures in the support of a community, like Alcoholics Anonymous. They struggle to find a more adult way to know God, sensing that their childhood vision of God no longer helps them as it once did.

In the collection *Morning Light*, the song "Well of Tears" offers a symbol of that shift. When planes fly into skyscrapers and buildings turn into rubble, people find hope in places where hope seems gone. For those willing to trust, God works in those burnt out places of our lives and, as at the beginning of time, creates something from nothing.

My hope for these songs is not around fame or financial success. I pray that they be worthy instruments with which God may touch people. If not, it's been a good ride, and I've grown.

Bob Dufford, S.J.

I do not experience the dawn very often, but when I do, especially from a vantage point, the transformation from dark to light presents itself as something quite mysterious. If you take time to notice it, dark has a kind of crystal quality about it, holding private what we do but shimmering with the promise of light.

Before dawn, there comes a feeling of daylight before you actually perceive it. Without realizing it, the texture of the landscape begins to emerge. Darkness no longer has complete sway. Those pinpoints of light you had been seeing in the night now begin to emerge as ordinary porch lights or headlights or lights in the front window. Then, suddenly and seemingly without cause, on its own majestic willpower alone, the great sun shows its upper rim in the east. You want to yell, "Look, there it is!" At last the source for all life has returned, and it is beyond spectacle. It is home.

God is just like that sunrise, and we must not let ourselves be fooled by the darkness in our lives and in the world. Almost without our noticing it, God's tender love makes its way above the dim horizon of our lives, and sheer gloom turns into trust and love.

You may say this is impossible. The St. Louis Jesuits' hymns are attempted answers to that shadowy statement. The new ones, in our reunion collection *Morning Light*, ask God to "Teach Us to Pray," summon us to "Come Home," tell us to view the full daylight of the "Saving Power of God" and request that we "Gather the People" in hope of the ever-steady, ever-warming and always-returning morning light of God's specific love for all of us.

John Foley, S.J.

The day we realize that hope is something we **do**, that "feeling hopeful" is hope's most shallow and fleeting expression, that its deepest reality is a discipline, a chosen practice, that we lay our hands to and put our backs behind like a well-worn tool — that's the day we touch the edge of hope as a virtue rather than a pastel word airbrushed on a greeting card.

It's what we do right here, right now, every day, to provide life for ourselves and the ones we love. Any "hope" that preaches a rejection of here and now for the promise of a hazy abstraction couched in terms of a "better" world, or a "better" church, or a "better" self, is not hope at all: it's a child's magical wish list. And it's a failure of religion in its old, deep meaning, of *re-ligio*, tying back in, the ancient task of staying connected, a failure finally to choose the notched axe, the leaky pail, and a body's good sweat as perfectly acceptable manifestations of Spirit always and everywhere in the act of **work**, of creating itself.

Of course, men and women have always sung while they worked. We've tried to help with that, with sometimes giving a voice, together, to the songs that rise from people working at staying awake, making a life. Now that, **that's** a hopeful sound.

Tim Manion

A revelation occurred to me when Bob, Dan, John and I sang "City of God" together at an OCP retrospective event at the 2001 National Pastoral Musicians' convention in Washington, DC. It was the first time we had sung together in sixteen years. I felt consolation from being together that differed from the kind and hearty applause from the people that afternoon. Singing together that day opened a door for me.

I pressed the others to find out whether they, too, felt something at that moment. We had been given a very consoling grace. None of us knew its meaning but at least we continued to ask the question and attempted to unravel some of the mystery of that moment of consolation. "What does this mean? Where does this grace point us?" I continued to pester the others. It all culminated in our meeting for several days of discernment in October 2003 at the University of San Francisco.

We asked, "Where do we see the state of the church today? What is the state of liturgy? What does the church need now? How might we respond?" We recognized a shared sense of mission and the meaning of liturgical prayer that was still alive. We spoke about our need for hope today. We reflected on the many changes in the church since the early 1960s. We considered the changing interpretations of what liturgical music the church should sing. Mostly we talked about our need for hope and the church's need for hope in difficult times.

All these questions and those days of discernment arose from those original moments when we sang together after a long period of working separately. The notion for putting together this collection, *Morning Light*, was conceived during those days. We wanted to offer the church a witness of reconciliation, an investment in an unknown future and our own desire to enter more deeply into the paschal mystery. We know that it is God's grace at work in us.

I really can't point to a specific hope for the church as we face an unknowable future. I can point to this one experience that we are playing out at this writing. I believe that we are being led, ever so slowly and in trust, by the spirit of God to offer this new collection of music as an act of hope in that future. On good days, I believe and acknowledge that this journey leads to and through the cross of Christ. One day the final resurrection to everlasting life will be the gift God gives.

Roc O'Connor, S.J.

At my core, I think I am a hopeful person, but I certainly know discouragement. The pain and tragedy of life has a way of eating away at our hopes and dreams. Like many, I am disheartened by the state of our world, by the religious and cultural intolerance and all the conflicts that arise from it. I am so saddened that we cannot seem to rejoice in our differences. I am sad that we keep trying to make others in our own image. While there are those who call this the age of relativism, there is a disheartening absolutism prevalent today that closes the door of dialogue in the face of those with opposing viewpoints. The church closed its ears to the voices of Joan of Arc, Galileo, Teilhard de Chardin, John Courtney Murray and John Henry Newman. I am very sad to know that there are those in the church that view the Second Vatican Council as a colossal mistake.

My novice master had a favorite expression that he'd preach to us. "Grow or die," he'd say. But growth often entails painful struggle and giving up the old ways we cling to for security. Some would say the institution of the church today is in crisis. At minimum, it has many painful challenges ahead. Why should the church that preaches the cross as being the way to life not experience great suffering and pain on her journey into life? I cling to the hope that what will rise from this crisis will be something wondrous and breathtakingly beautiful. "Behold, I make all things new" (Revelation 21:5).

St. Paul preaches that the greatest sin is the sin against the Holy Spirit. I understand him to mean the sin of giving in to the temptation of despair, of no longer believing that the Breath of God guides our lives and is at work in the church and in our earth's tragedies and triumphs. The faith of my later years clings to my belief in God's Indwelling Spirit.

Dan Schutte

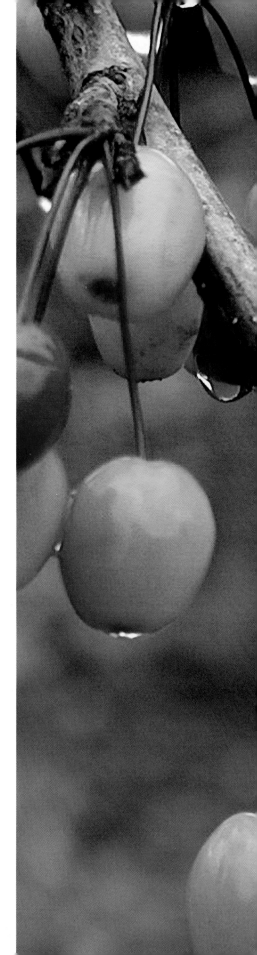

Take, Lord, and receive all my liberty,
my memory, understanding, my entire will,
all that I have and call my own.
You have given all to me.
To you, Lord, I return it.
Do with it as you will.
Give me only your love and your grace;
that is enough for me.

St. Ignatius of Loyola